AS/A-LEVEL YEAR 1

STUDENT GUIDE

OCR

Sociology

Researching and understanding social inequalities

Steve Chapman

ANDOVER COLLEGE

PHILIP ALLAN FOR
HODDER
EDUCATION
AN HACHETTE UK COMPANY

Philip Allan, an imprint of Hodder Education, an Hachette UK company, Blenheim Court, George Street, Banbury, Oxfordshire OX16 5BH

Orders

Bookpoint Ltd, 130 Park Drive, Milton Park, Abingdon, Oxfordshire OX14 4SB

tel: 01235 827827

fax: 01235 400401

e-mail: education@bookpoint.co.uk

Lines are open 9.00 a.m.–5.00 p.m., Monday to Saturday, with a 24-hour message answering service. You can also order through the Hodder Education website: www.hoddereducation.co.uk

© Steve Chapman 2016

ISBN 978-1-4718-4429-4

First printed 2016

Impression number 5 4 3 2 1

Year 2020 2019 2018 2017 2016

This Guide has been written specifically to support students preparing for the OCR AS and A-level Sociology examinations. The content has been neither approved nor endorsed by OCR and remains the sole responsibility of the author.

Cover photo: thakala/Fotolia

Typeset by Integra Software Services Pvt. Ltd., Pondicherry, India

Printed in Italy

Hachette UK's policy is to use papers that are natural, renewable and recyclable products and made from wood grown in sustainable forests. The logging and manufacturing processes are expected to conform to the environmental regulations of the country of origin.

Contents

Content Guidance

Questions & Answers

■ Getting the most from this book

Exam-style questions

Commentary on the questions

Tips on what you need to do to gain full marks, indicated by the icon **e**

Sample student answers

Practise the questions, then look at the student answers that follow.

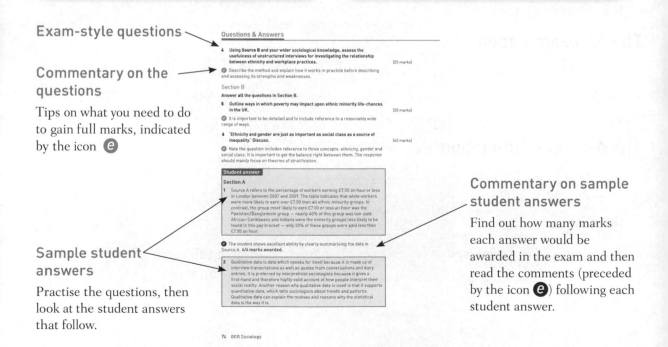

Commentary on sample student answers

Find out how many marks each answer would be awarded in the exam and then read the comments (preceded by the icon **e**) following each student answer.

■ About this book

This guide covers Component 2: Researching and understanding social inequalities in the OCR Sociology specifications H180 (AS) and H580 (A-level). The content is identical for both, but A-level students will be expected to demonstrate a greater knowledge and understanding of sociological theory. The structure of the examination is also different for AS and A-level, so when you come to read through the questions, it is important that you note which are the correct ones for your course, though you may, of course, wish to use the others for revision or exam practice.

How to use the book

The first main section of the book is **Content Guidance**. It follows the headings for Researching and understanding social inequalities in the OCR specification. Each section of the Content Guidance contains exam tips, knowledge checks and definitions of some key terms. Knowing and understanding the meaning of sociological concepts is an essential part of the whole course.

The second main section of the book is **Questions & Answers**. At the beginning of this section are the three assessment objectives against which your exam answers will be judged, with some guidance regarding how to display the required skills, and also a list of command words, which will help you to understand more clearly what each question is asking you to do. The questions provided are in the style of the OCR exam for Component 2 and are divided into AS and A-level questions, each followed by an A-grade answer. Remember the importance of noting the structure and mark allocations of questions at the appropriate level for you, either AS or A-level. However, given that the content is the same, there is no harm in writing answers to all the questions given here — just remember when you look at the marks awarded and read the comments that they are being applied to a particular level, either AS or A-level. Throughout the student answers, you will find comments, explaining why what has been written is good and is scoring well. More detailed guidance on how to use the Questions & Answers section is given at the beginning of that section.

Content Guidance

■ Section A Research methods and researching social inequalities

What is the relationship between theory and methods?

Key research concepts

Validity

Validity is a concept that generally refers to whether research and its findings give a true picture of what is being studied, that is, whether research reflects the reality of the activities or attitudes of the person/group being studied. Validity is important to all sociologists but especially important to those researchers known as interpretivists who want to understand the motives and meanings that people attach to their actions.

However, validity can be undermined by a number of factors:

- First, the results of research can sometimes be the product of poor research design rather than a reflection of the social situation being studied.
- Second, the research subjects may sometimes lie to or mislead researchers or quite simply tell them what they think he or she would like to hear.
- Third, people may change their behaviour because they are anxious about being the subject of research.
- Fourth, the researcher may misinterpret the behaviour or words of the research subjects.

Reliability

Reliability is a concept usually applied to the way the research or measurement process is designed. If the research design is reliable, it generally means that if it is used by other researchers on a similar group of people, the same or similar results should be produced. Reliability is particularly important to sociologists known as positivists who want to carry out scientific research and who wish to generate data that can be quantified and compared in order to uncover correlations or cause-and-effect relationships.

However, reliability may be undermined by the fact that some types of research methods, notably unstructured interviews and participant observation, often depend on the quality of the personal relationship established between the researcher and the research subjects. It may be impossible for other sociologists to replicate these unique relationships.

> **Exam tip**
>
> Make sure you go into the exam with a clear definition of validity and an illustration. Do not make the common error of confusing it with reliability.

> **Knowledge check 1**
>
> Why do some sociologists argue that reliability is overrated as a component of the scientific method?

Representativeness

Sociologists are often interested in how social groups behave or think. However, some social groups are so large it is impractical and too expensive to include every member of that group in the research. Sociologists therefore research samples of the larger social group. Nevertheless, it is important that the sample is representative, that is, it is made up of people who mirror the characteristics of the larger population in terms of social class, age, gender, ethnicity etc. If the researcher fails to ensure that the group participating in the research is representative, then bias may result and the data collected may be invalid.

Generalisability

Sociologists use representative samples because they normally want to generalise about the behaviour and attitudes of a larger group, of which the sample is a typical cross-section. They want to say that because the sample behaves or thinks in a particular way, it is highly likely that people similar to those included in the sample will also behave/think in this way. However, critics argue that even if people share the same social characteristics, this is no guarantee that they will interpret the same social situation in a similar way.

Positivism

Positivists argue that social behaviour and therefore society is the product of social forces beyond the control of the individual. The origin of these social forces or laws lies in the way societies are organised, that is, their social structure. Positivists argue that the social structure produces social forces such as **consensus**, **integration**, social class, patriarchy and so on that shape or determine the behaviour of human beings. In this way, people are the puppets of society.

Positivists highlight the predictability of human actions by identifying social patterns and trends in social actions. For example, they note that the mass of working-class people generally behave in similar ways with regard to family life, educational achievement, consumption of consumer goods, leisure and cultural pursuits and so on to the extent that there are very clear working-class patterns of behaviour that contrast greatly with middle-class or upper-class social behaviour.

Positivists believe that society and the social forces that underpin it should be studied using scientific research methods. There are a number of principles that underpin this scientific approach.

Patterns and trends

First, research should be designed so that it is standardised, systematic and logical. All those who take part in the research should be equally exposed to the same potential independent variable (for example, questions) in order to uncover the cause of their behaviour/attitudes. This aspect of research design should ensure reliability.

Objectivity and value freedom

Second, it is important that the research is carried out in an objective fashion to ensure that bias does not undermine the research findings. Value freedom is the idea that all sources of bias have been eliminated from the research process. For example, the research design needs to ensure that if the researcher is using a questionnaire or

Exam tip

Examiners will reward successful attempts to link the strengths and weaknesses of research methods to the concepts of reliability, validity and representativeness.

Consensus Refers to the sharing of agreement, for example that some belief is worth pursuing.

Integration Refers to a sense of belonging to a group or society.

Exam tip

It is important to remember that the theories of functionalism, Marxism and feminism have this positivist approach to human behaviour in common.

interview, the questions are neutral — they should not reflect any personal, moral, political or sociological position that might lead research subjects into giving only certain responses. The researcher also needs to ensure that their interpretation of data is objective — they should avoid being selective when analysing and evaluating their data.

However, the notion of value freedom is a contentious one because critics argue that sociology is social knowledge that is underpinned by sociological perspectives, moral codes, prejudices and therefore bias. For example, most sociology reflects Western, capitalist and patriarchal values. Sociology is therefore composed of values because sociologists are members of society and thus cannot escape the influence of its culture and its institutions.

Quantitative data

Third, positivists are very keen on the collection and use of quantitative or numerical data that can be converted into graphs, tables and charts, which allow them to identify correlations between patterns and trends. Statistics are viewed as the objective result of the scientific process and are regarded as essential in the identification of the social forces (**independent variables**) which positivists argue are the main influence on the behaviour of individuals (**dependent variable**).

Positivist sociologists prefer to use social surveys that employ questionnaires and/or structured interviews as their primary research method because these supposedly are scientific in character. However, they are also keen to use official statistics because these are normally the result of standardised, reliable and objective research and/or data collection.

Interpretivism or social action theory

Interpretivists do not believe that human behaviour is predictable or that it is shaped by social laws or social forces over which people have no control. They argue that people have free will and can therefore exercise choice and make decisions to pursue their own courses of action. Individuals are therefore active rather than passive. They create their own destinies rather than having them shaped by social structures. They are architects of society rather than puppets.

Meanings and experiences

Interpretivists consider the social world to be socially constructed — it is the product of shared interaction and the meanings or interpretations that humans use to make sense of that interaction. The role of sociologists is to uncover these shared interpretations or meanings, to document social experience and identify the motives and reasons for social actions.

Verstehen, empathy and rapport

Interpretivists argue that the aim of sociological research should be to get inside people's heads and to experience the world from their point of view. This is called empathetic understanding or **verstehen**. They therefore emphasise the use of ethnographic methods such as unstructured interviews and participant observation, which aim to conduct research in the research subject's natural environment and to establish a rapport or trust between the sociologist and the research subject. This approach stresses that the validity of the research data is more important than reliability.

Exam tip
The notion that value freedom is virtually impossible to achieve is important when discussing the relationship between sociology and social policy.

Independent variable The cause of something.

Dependent variable The effect of something.

Knowledge check 2
Who or what is responsible for society and the actions of its members according to positivist sociologists?

Knowledge check 3
Who or what is responsible for society and the actions of its members according to interpretivist sociologists?

Verstehen An important concept that refers to the ability of the social researcher to get inside the head of the research subject and to understand the social world and action from their perspective using methods such as unstructured interviews, participant observation and diaries.

Qualitative data

Interpretivists are not that keen on quantitative data because they believe it tells researchers little about feelings, experiences or reasons for behaviour. They also believe that such data is socially constructed and therefore it may reflect the biases of the groups involved in its collection.

Interpretivists prefer qualitative data. This is data that speaks for itself because it is made up of personal accounts taken directly from the subjects of sociological research in the form of interview transcriptions, quotes from conversations that occur as part of the process of participant observations, diary entries and so on. This data tends to focus on how the research subjects see or interpret the world around them and consequently it often provides insight into the feelings, opinions, motivations and thoughts of those being researched. It allows those being studied to speak for themselves.

Exam tip

Much of the debate about the strengths and weaknesses of research methods reflects the debate about whether to take a positivist or interpretivist approach to the investigation of social life. Work this positivist–interpretivist distinction into your answers whenever you can.

Subjectivity, researcher imposition and reflexivity

Interpretivists argue that researcher imposition is an important source of bias in positivist sociological research, that is, when developing research tools, researchers often make decisions or have assumptions about what is and is not important based on their own experience rather than that of the research subjects. Consequently they may miss something important.

Interpretivists argue that their approach of putting the research subjects at the centre of the research avoids this problem. However, critics point out that there is always the danger in research involving the establishment of rapport and close relationships with subjects that the sociologist may 'go native' and allow their subjective relationships to overcome their detachment and objectivity. There is also the danger that subjectivity might intrude into the research process in the form of selective interpretation of the data because the researcher sympathises with the lifestyle of the group being studied.

Knowledge check 4

Why might interpretivist methods be seen by positivists as unreliable?

However, interpretivist sociologists tend to be aware of this possibility of bias and have stressed the importance of reflexivity. This refers to researchers being aware of how their decisions and actions may impact on the social behaviour of their subjects during the research process. In order to improve the validity of their findings, many researchers keep a journal or diary of the research process in which they critically self-reflect on their research design and everyday experience of contact with their subjects.

Interpretivist sociologists prefer to use research methods such as unstructured interviews and overt/covert participant observation, which allow sociologists access to the everyday world of research subjects. Nevertheless, they are also keen to use secondary sources of data such as diaries, biographies, autobiographies and so on because these focus on how specific individuals interpret their everyday social reality.

Summary

- There are two important approaches to choosing a research method: positivism and interpretivism.
- Positivists believe that social behaviour is largely the product of social forces that originate in the social structure or organisation of society.
- Positivists believe that sociologists should use scientific methods that are standardised, reliable and objectively value-free.
- They use methods such as questionnaire surveys and structured interviews which use representative samples and produce quantitative data.
- In contrast, interpretivists reject the idea that people are the puppets of society.

- Interpretivists believe that social behaviour is the result of people actively choosing to interact in social groups and the interpretations or social meanings that people apply to those encounters.
- Interpretivists stress the concept of validity, that is, research methods should be ethnographic in order to produce qualitative data that reflects true, authentic and natural behaviour as well as achieving verstehen, that is, seeing the world through the eyes of those being studied by the sociologist.
- Interpretivists therefore prefer methods such as unstructured interviews and participant observation.

What are the main stages of the research process?

Key concepts in the research process

Factors influencing the choice of research topic

The choice of research method is likely to be influenced by several practical issues.

Costs

Research plans, i.e. what to research, how to research and the size of the research team, are dependent on the economic resources available. Large-scale research projects are expensive, for example, the costs of such research are likely to include the salaries of the research team and the secretarial help, equipment such as computers, travel and so on. The employment and training of a large interviewing team, or a long-term participant observation (that is, living alongside or among the social group being studied for months or years), will require substantial funds. If financial resources are low, a survey using postal questionnaires may be more practical than methods that involve employing several people.

Funding

The problems of cost may be eased if the research is funded by social institutions that can pay salaries or offer grants. A student carrying out sociological research for a dissertation is likely to use a cheap research method such as a questionnaire on a limited sample of people because they do not have access to funding. However, many sociologists are funded by their university departments, the Economic and Social Research Council, government departments, think-tanks and social policy research charities such as the Joseph Rowntree Foundation. These sociologists are likely to be more ambitious in the scope and design of their research. For example, they may be able to afford to use national samples of thousands of people, to recruit large teams of interviewers and to use a variety of research tools.

However, their research may also be shaped by the funding body. For example, those financing the research may demand quantitative data as the outcome because they wish to highlight certain trends and patterns. This demand for statistics will obviously restrict the researcher to a choice of questionnaires and structured interviews. However, some funding bodies may wish for qualitative data that documents first-hand the daily experience of, say, living in poverty, which then gives the researcher scope for using research methods such as unstructured interviews and participant observation.

Time

The time scale may be an important factor in the choice of method. If the time scale is short, a survey questionnaire may be used because questionnaires can be designed, sent out and returned within a month. Structured interviews, too, can be conducted very quickly. However, if the researcher has the funding for long-term research they may choose to use ethnographic methods. It takes time to develop the trust and rapport that produce the qualitative data that comes from unstructured interviews when observing the lives of particular groups, while living among them on a daily basis may take several years. Even if the researcher chooses to use a survey method, they may decide that they have the funding and time to conduct a longitudinal study that involves revisiting the research subjects over a period of years to document how their situation has changed.

The nature of the subject matter

Some topics are sensitive and people may be reluctant to admit to behaviour such as domestic violence, racism, crime or sexual activity when face to face with an interviewer. Yet they may be prepared to answer questions on these topics if a questionnaire guarantees them anonymity and confidentiality. Some sociologists may choose to go undercover and use covert participant observation to investigate certain types of crime and deviance that would not normally be open to researchers because criminals equate questionnaires and interviews with officialdom. Some researchers may be forced into using particular methods because the subject matter excludes other methods. For example, if the subject matter is illiteracy, the chosen research method is unlikely to be questionnaires.

The social characteristics of the researchers

The social characteristics of the researcher(s) and particularly their status in the eyes of those being researched must be considered if research is to be successful. Social class, gender, age, ethnicity, accents, dress, personality etc. are all factors that may impact positively or negatively on the choice of research method. For example, white middle-class researchers interested in the everyday experience of poverty experienced by black and Asian people may find that participant observation is unlikely to be successful and that they may not be able to establish the trust and rapport required to produce successful unstructured interviews.

Aims, hypothesis and research questions

Stage one of the research process is to decide on the topic, issue or social problem that is going to be researched and the research method that is going to be used. The most common research methods used by sociologists are: survey questionnaires; various types of interviews, particularly the structured, unstructured and group forms; various types of observation, especially direct observation and participant

Knowledge check 5

Why might funding undermine the objectivity of sociological research?

Knowledge check 6

Why might the subject matter undermine the validity of the data collected by sociological research?

Exam tip

Examiners are fond of asking about the influence of these practical factors on research, but remember that researchers are just as influenced by theoretical and ethical factors.

forms of observation; and either content or semiotic analysis of mass media content. Experiments are also a possibility, but sociologists rarely use them because they throw up a range of practical and ethical problems.

Stage two of the research is to read what others have published on the subject in order to avoid repeating what somebody else has already done. Such reading may give the researcher ideas about how to approach the topic or issue.

Stage three involves constructing a hypothesis. This is an informed guess that something is true. It is usually based on previous sociological research and knowledge rather than being a random gut feeling. A hypothesis usually takes the form of a statement or a set of aims or research questions that can be tested. It is a prediction of what the research will find. However, in some types of sociological research studies, the researcher does not have a clear hypothesis, but starts with a general aim and develops the hypothesis and research questions as the data collection proceeds.

Primary and secondary data

Stage four involves deciding whether to exclusively collect primary data or secondary data or a combination of both.

Primary data is gathered 'first-hand' by the sociologist using a variety of methods, for example:

- asking people questions via questionnaires or interviews
- observing their behaviour
- conducting experiments.

Secondary data is data that has been collected or produced by people who are not sociologists. For example, official statistics relating to the life-chances of specific social classes, ethnic groups and men and women are collected by the government. Journalists may research poverty or inequality and publish their findings in the form of a newspaper or magazine article.

Operationalisation

Stage five of the research process involves the researcher breaking down the hypothesis and the aims that result from this into something that can be observed or measured. For example, any concepts in the hypothesis must be broken down into questions or observable categories. This process is known as 'operationalisation'. For example, the hypothesis 'Working-class people are less likely to experience upward social mobility' gives rise to three questions of operationalisation:

- What is meant by 'working-class'? This is the research population to be studied so it is important to be precise as to who should be included in this group.
- Are 'less likely' than who? It is important to precisely identify the social group that will be compared with the research population.
- What is meant by 'upward social mobility'? It is important to identify a range of indicators of upward social mobility.

Operationalisation of concepts is an important part of the research process. Precise measurement of social phenomena cannot occur without it. Positivists prefer it as it assists reliability because other researchers can use the same operationalisation criteria. It also aids objectivity because the operationalisation process should weed out

Exam tip

Operationalisation refers to the practical process of turning a hypothesis or research aim into something that can be observed and quantified. For example, social class can be quantified by asking about people's jobs, incomes, lifestyles etc. via a questionnaire or interview.

potential bias, for example in the design of the questions. Finally, it should ensure that validity is achieved in terms of the data gathered because operationalisation should establish what the sociologist is setting out to measure.

Data collection

Stage six involves choosing the type of data required. The researchers may prefer quantitative data, that is, factual data in the form of numbers or statistics which can be displayed in various ways, such as tables, graphs, bar charts, pie charts, tally charts, columns of figures and lists of percentages.

Some researchers prefer qualitative data, which provides a richly descriptive and personal account of the social world, often in the actual words of those being studied. The worldview of the research subjects in terms of their experiences, attitudes, interpretations, motives for behaviour and so on may be selected for use from interview transcripts or accounts of conversations that have taken place during participant observation or from diaries that the research team has asked the research subjects to keep to document their daily activities.

Most sociological research tends to combine both primary and secondary forms of data, that is, quantitative data is collected to show the facts, for example, the patterns and trends, that support (or challenge) the hypothesis while qualitative evidence adds a human dimension as to how the research subjects actually experience and interpret the social processes highlighted by the hypothesis.

Pilot studies

Stage seven of the research process involves testing the reliability of the research design and therefore hopefully improving the validity of the data eventually collected.

Most sociologists intending to use a questionnaire or interviews will carry out pilot studies in order to iron out any potential problems with the questions and/or the ways interviews are conducted. Pilot studies are therefore a dress rehearsal for the main research and are tested on a relatively small number of people who have similar characteristics to those who will constitute the main sample. A pilot study is useful because it can check:

- whether questions are clear and unambiguous and that those taking part are interpreting the questions in the same way
- that the questions do not upset or lead the participants in giving particular types of responses that may bias the outcome of the research findings
- that the research design has successfully identified the 'right' types of people as the research subjects
- that the interviewers are well trained and not biasing the data by the way they respond to the research subjects
- that the data produced is the kind that is wanted.

Respondent validation

Respondent validation is a method used by some sociologists to double-check the validity of behaviour that they might have observed the research subjects displaying. It is sometimes used to check whether the sociological interpretation of why certain attitudes have been expressed on a questionnaire or during an interview is supported by those who have expressed such feelings.

Knowledge check 7

What approach to research prefers qualitative rather than quantitative data?

....

Exam tip

It is important that you are able to identify the seven stages of the research process in sequence. Invent some sort of mnemonic sentence to help you learn the stages: PRHDOCP — *Prince* (Problem to be investigated), *Rupert* (Reading previous research), *Henry* (Hypothesis), *Dismisses* (Data — primary or secondary?), *Old* (operationalisation), *Crown* (Choice of quantitative or qualitative data), *Prince* (Pilot study). You might be able to come up with a more memorable version.

....

It is based on the acknowledgement that sociologists often come from different backgrounds to the people they are studying and that their upbringing and education may mean they are ill-equipped to understand the behaviour they are researching. It is also a response to a common critique of sociological research that the sociologist often ends up imposing their interpretation of reality on the behaviour of the group being studied. Respondent validation aims to address these problems that potentially undermine validity.

Respondent validation aims to improve the authenticity of the collected data by asking a sample of the research subjects whether the sociological interpretation of their behaviour and motives equates with the reality of why they behaved in the way they did. Research subjects are invited to answer further questions, perhaps as part of a follow-up, unstructured interview, or, if the research is observation-based, the observer may engage a person in an informal conversation in an attempt to understand the motives for that person's behaviour.

Knowledge check 8

What approach to research is most likely to adopt respondent validation?

Longitudinal studies

Some sociological research is longitudinal in nature. This means that it is carried out over a long period of years, for example, participant observation studies have been known to last 7–8 years, or that the research team revisits the same research subjects on an annual basis for a number of years to carry out questionnaires, surveys or interviews.

Such surveys are useful because they can provide a clear image of changes in attitudes and behaviour over a number of years. For example, the National Child Development Study has followed the same 40,000 children all born in one week in March 1958. Follow-up surveys have tracked the group at the ages of 16, 23 and 33 and given sociologists fascinating insights into the influence of class, education and family on life-chances. However, such surveys can be problematic:

a Respondents may drop out or die or the researchers may lose track of them. This may undermine the representativeness of the original sample.

b The views of those that remain in the sample may be significantly different to those of the subjects that drop out. This may undermine both the reliability and the validity of the research.

c There is a danger that the research team over time gets too emotionally close to the group and consequently may lose its ability to be objective.

Exam tip

It is important to remember that longitudinal studies are a type of social survey. This means you can include them in any discussion of the merits of surveys in general.

Interpretation of data

Positivist sociologists believe it is important that the interpretation of data should be carried out in an objective fashion and that data should not be selected simply because it supports the hypothesis. The sociologist should therefore also unbiasedly include all data in their published findings, even if this challenges their hypothesis. Positivists believe that research that mainly uses quantitative data is more likely to achieve this objective than research that focuses mainly on qualitative data because it is argued that the latter involves more subjective and therefore potentially biased interpretation from the sociologist. The use of respondent validation and reflexivity is a response to this critique.

The relationship between sociology and social policy

Social policy generally refers to attempts by governments to influence how society is organised and how members of society should behave by bringing in new laws, guidelines and controls. Social policy is often aimed at bringing about social change. This change may have profound immediate effects (e.g. the government introduced a free National Health Service overnight in 1948) or it may have a more gradual influence (e.g. the government often tinkers with the education system).

Sociologists play an important part in helping social policymakers formulate social policy because they collect evidence relating to two types of problem that often result in the need for social policy. First, sociologists are interested in explaining and solving social problems, that is, behaviour that causes misery and conflict such as poverty, inequality, unemployment, racism, crime, divorce and so on. Second, sociologists are interested in explaining sociological problems, that is, why society and the social institutions that make it up are organised in the way they are. Some of these sociological problems are social problems, but many are positive processes that are beneficial to society. For example, the sociologist is just as interested in why people in the UK are motivated to marry as they are in why people get divorced. The evidence collected by sociologists with regard to both social and sociological problems therefore often underpins the rationale for social policy.

There are essentially two perspectives with regard to the relationship between sociology and social policy. The first suggests that the job of sociologists is to merely collect evidence on behalf of social policymakers but it is no concern of the sociologist how that data is used. We have to trust that the social policymaker uses the sociological data for the good of all members of society and even if they do not, sociologists do not have the moral responsibility to ensure social policymakers use the data properly. From this perspective, sociologists are merely disinterested and objective pursuers of facts and truth.

In contrast, the second perspective suggests that sociologists need to take responsibility for how their work is translated into social policy because society is characterised by conflicts of interest between different social groups. Some of these wield tremendous power and may be the cause of the social problems identified by sociologists, therefore some sociologists have argued that the point of sociology is not just to interpret the world but to challenge its organisation and change it for the better.

The sampling process

It is usually too expensive and time-consuming to ask everybody in a research population to take part in research. Most researchers select a sample that is representative (i.e. a typical cross-section) of the population they are interested in. With a representative sample, it is possible to generalise to the wider research population, that is, what is true of the sample should be true of the research population as a whole.

There are two main sampling techniques available to sociologists: random sampling and non-random sampling.

Exam tip

Most social policy is concerned with tackling or solving social problems such as crime or poverty. Make sure you are able to illustrate how this works by equipping yourself with three or four examples of such policies from areas such as family or crime.

Knowledge check 9

Which theoretical approach to research — positivism or interpretivism— do you think would be sympathetic to the idea that sociologists are merely objective pursuers of truth?

Knowledge check 10

Which sociological theories would agree that the point of sociological research is to change the world for the better?

Exam tip

Make sure you equip yourself with examples that you can use to illustrate these two sides of the debate.

Random sampling techniques

Random sampling

A simple random sample involves selecting names randomly from a sampling frame, which is a list of names such as the electoral register, the postcode address file, school or college attendance registers, GP patient records and so on. Using this technique, every member of the research population has an equal chance of being included in the sample, so those chosen are likely to be a cross-section of the population.

All sampling frames are unsatisfactory in some respect — not everyone is included, they are often out of date and some groups may be over-represented while other groups may not be included. Also, a simple random sample may not guarantee a representative sample — a researcher may select too many young people, too many males, not enough members of poorer groups such as the homeless etc. Sociologists have therefore developed two variations on the random sample in order to produce representative samples:

Systematic sampling

This involves randomly choosing a number between 1 and 10, e.g. 7, and then identifying every tenth number from that point, e.g. 7, 17, 27, 37, from the sampling frame until the sample is complete. This does not always guarantee a representative sample, but the larger the sample, the more likely it is to be representative.

Stratified sampling

This technique is the most common form of random sampling used in sociological research. It involves dividing the sampling frames into a number of sampling categories. For example, if researchers were sampling students at a college and discovered that 60% of students were female and 40% were male, they would want their sample to reflect those proportions. The sampling frame, i.e. college registers, would need to be transformed into the two gender categories, that is, a list of female students and a list of male students. If the researchers intended to have an overall sample of 100 students, they could then randomly select 60 female and 40 male students from their two lists. Researchers could, if necessary, construct sampling categories from sampling frames which would allow them to differentiate a sample based on age, ethnicity, social class and so on.

Non-random sampling techniques

Non-random sampling techniques may be used instead of random techniques for both practical and theoretical reasons. Sometimes no suitable sampling frame is available to the research team. For example, there is unlikely to be a sampling frame that lists the names of the homeless. Some people may refuse to cooperate with formal research because they are engaged in deviant activity. Some interpretivist sociologists do not see the need for random sampling because they are interested in the specific experience of particular small-scale groups located in specific locations, for example homeless people who use a particular hostel.

Snowball sampling

This type of sampling is used mainly when it is difficult to gain access to a particular group of people because there is no sampling frame available or because they engage

Exam tip

The examiner may ask you to define what is meant by a sampling frame. Make sure you can illustrate your definition with a practical example.

in deviant or illegal activities that are normally carried out in isolation or in secret. This technique involves finding and interviewing a person who fits the research needs and then asking him/her to suggest another person who might be willing to be interviewed. The sample can grow as large as the researcher wants. Plant used this type of sampling technique in his study of cannabis use. However, snowball sampling may produce an atypical sample because those who agree to take part are unlikely to be representative of the wider group to which they belong.

Volunteer sampling

People may be asked to volunteer to take part in research because no sampling frame is available or because the subject matter may focus on a research question that may be too embarrassing for a wider audience and therefore result in a high level of non-response or refusal. However, this is regarded as the weakest form of sampling since the participants may have volunteered because they have their own agenda or motives that conflict with the aims of the research.

Opportunity sampling

Opportunity sampling involves researchers choosing individuals who (or cases that) are available at the time of the study and fit the nature of the research. For example, a researcher interested in how skateboarders in Leeds see themselves might visit a local skate park over a weekend and ask all those present to take part in the research.

Purposive sampling

Purposive sampling is when a researcher chooses specific people within the population to use for a particular study or research project. Usually, the researcher is not interested in a diverse research population. Rather they will want to focus on people with particular characteristics who will be better able to assist with the relevant research. For example, research on single mothers who are claiming benefits logically would look to sample precisely that group rather than mothers in general or single mothers who are not claiming benefits because they would be unable to relate anything relevant to the study.

Quota sampling

This technique is used by market researchers who target particular types of people in the street. In other words, such researchers are given quotas of people to fulfil, that is, they may be asked to interview 30 housewives about a particular consumer product or 100 people aged between 18 and 25 about their voting preferences.

Access and gate-keeping

Sociological researchers need to think carefully about how they are going to access the institution in which their research group is mostly likely to be found. Access to some groups may be relatively straightforward. For example, if the research is focused on teenagers, this group is most likely to be found in a school. Researchers could gain access to this group by writing to local education authorities and head teachers for permission to enter schools. Registers could act as sampling frames. However, if the research wanted to focus on children under the age of 16, parental informed consent would need to be sought.

> **Exam tip**
>
> It is important to understand that sampling is a technique that helps sociologists to recruit people to take part in their research. Do not make the mistake of referring to sampling as a research method.

Other groups may be quite difficult to access. For example, there is no sampling frame for the elderly and the researcher may be forced to use non-random methods such as approaching a quota of elderly people in the street or opportunity sampling at social events for the elderly.

Some sociologists have accessed particular groups via the internet, e.g. through chat rooms or interactive sites such as Facebook and even Twitter. This is especially useful for research situations that are potentially embarrassing and off-putting if carried out face to face. Some researchers have even set up interactive research sites where they post notices asking for volunteers, or questionnaires for internet users to complete.

A big problem for sociologists is that some groups have the power to deny access to sociologists. This is probably the main reason why there are few sociological studies of institutions, such as private schools, big businesses and so on, and why there are a lots of sociological studies of state schools and people who are relatively powerless, such as the poor and unemployed.

If a sociologist wants to access a group using participant observation they will need to share the social characteristics of the group. However, some groups do not want to be studied because they are engaged in deviant or criminal activity. Access to criminals is particularly problematic. The researcher could seek permission to carry out their research with convicted criminals but this sample may not be representative of typical criminals. Some sociologists have managed to insinuate themselves into deviant or criminal worlds as participant observers by offering a service to the group or its leader or by being sponsored by a gate-keeper, that is, a trusted member of the group who reassures the group of the legitimacy of the newcomer and that they pose no threat to the group.

Knowledge check 11

Why might using the internet to access a sample be problematical for sociological research?

Ethics

The British Sociological Association argues that ethical issues are important because research can have a powerful impact on people's lives. It insists therefore that researchers must always think carefully about the impact of their research. Researchers need to acknowledge that research subjects have rights and that researchers have responsibilities and obligations towards them. Generally, British sociologists agree that the following broad ethical rules should underpin all sociological research:

a Informed consent: many researchers believe that all research participants have a right to know what the research is about and the right to refuse to take part or to answer particular questions. People should know that research is being carried out on them and how the results will be used so that they can make an informed choice as to whether they should take part. Deception in any shape or form therefore needs to be avoided. However, informed consent is not always a straightforward matter. For example, very young children or people with learning disabilities may not be able to understand fully what the researcher is doing.

Not all sociologists agree that this is a rule worth following. Interpretivist sociologists who use covert forms of observation depend upon deception for the success of their research, which would not be possible if their research subjects were informed that the research was taking place. This is because these groups tend to be involved in deviant behaviour and in normal circumstances would not be willing to cooperate with a sociological study. In these cases, interpretivists argue that deception is outweighed by the validity of the data gathered, which gives insight into why such deviance occurs. For example, Humphreys carried out a covert observation study of homosexuality in which he deceived the participants as to his own sexuality and inclinations. However, he claimed that this deception was worth it because the results of his study improved public and official understanding of homosexuality and therefore reduced prejudice and discrimination towards this group.

b   Privacy and confidentiality: most sociologists agree that the privacy of research subjects should be safeguarded as much as possible. However, sociological research is by its very nature intrusive — sociologists are generally interested in what goes on in private and intimate social situations. The problem of maintaining privacy can be countered by keeping the identity of research participants secret. Confidentiality means that the information an individual gives to the researcher cannot be traced back to that individual. Ethical researchers are therefore careful to disguise the identity of individual participants when they write up their research. If participants know they cannot be identified, they may be more willing to reveal personal and private matters. In other words, confidentiality may increase the validity of the data collected.

c   Protection from harm: most sociologists agree that research participants should be protected from any sort of physical harm and this is seldom a problem. However, some sociological research may harm participants emotionally and psychologically by asking insensitive questions or by reminding them of some traumatic experience. Sociological research may also have harmful social consequences. For example, people's reputations may be damaged or they may be exposed to ridicule because of something a sociologist has published.

d   Legality and immorality: sociologists should avoid being drawn into situations where they may commit crimes or assist/witness deviant acts. If they come into possession of so-called 'guilty knowledge' such as information about crimes committed or about to be committed, it is suggested that this should be reported to the relevant authorities. However, interpretivist sociologists argue that if sociologists investigating deviant groups were to adopt this ethical rule, it would undermine the trust and rapport between the sociologist and research subjects and consequently seriously undermine the validity of the research.

Exam tip

Any question on the practical or theoretical factors that influence a sociologist's choice of research subject or method must include reference to ethical factors because these too are an influence.

Summary

- The choice of research method and subject is influenced not only by theoretical factors but also by a range of practical factors.
- The research hypothesis and aims must be operationalised, that is, broken down into components such as questions that can be measured and quantified.
- The design and/or progress of a research project can be tested by using pilot surveys or respondent validation.
- Sociologists make a big contribution to social policy, but there is disagreement as to how involved sociologists should be with social policymakers.
- It is usually impractical to study the whole of the population sociologists are interested in and therefore they tend to use sampling frames and random sampling techniques in order to choose samples that are representative of the larger group.
- If sampling frames are unavailable, sociologists might use non-random sampling techniques to gather suitable people to be researched.
- There are various ethical guidelines that sociologists are expected to follow.

Which methods are used in sociological research?

Research methods

Questionnaires

Questionnaires are composed of standardised lists of questions that result from operationalising a hypothesis. They normally form part of a social or sample survey, which means they aim to gather a large quantity of research data, usually quantitative data, from large groups of people who may be situated in the same place or be geographically scattered. They are normally distributed by hand or through the post, although they are sometimes distributed through mass media publications such as newspapers and magazines and posted on websites. Questionnaires are normally accompanied by a statement from the sociologist that outlines the aims of the research. If the person is happy to proceed (this indicates informed consent) they will complete and return the questionnaire to the researcher.

Questionnaire design can be a tricky business because the sociologist needs to ensure the following:

- The questions need to be focused on operationalising the key components of the hypothesis or research question.
- The questions need to be asked in a clear and simple way and avoid technical and/ or vague vocabulary so that they are not misunderstood or misinterpreted by the research subjects.
- Questions must be free of bias — they must not '**lead**' respondents into giving the answers that support the hypothesis, nor should they be '**loaded**' and/or provoke emotional responses that undermine validity because the research subject wants to evade either the truth or moral judgement about their behaviour.
- The questionnaire should be relatively short in order to avoid alienating the research subject. The subject may not complete it or send it back if it seems like hard work.

Leading questions
Biased because the way they are worded shapes the response, for example, 'Don't you think sex before marriage is disgusting' is likely to provoke a yes response because people wish to avoid being seen as 'disgusting'.

Loaded questions
Biased, poorly designed questions that nearly always elicit a negative emotional response, for example, 'Do you hit your children?'

- Most questionnaires normally use 'closed' questions. This is a question that is accompanied by a number of categories. The respondent is asked to tick the category that most applies to their social characteristics (e.g. male or female), their behaviour and their attitudes, beliefs, experiences and so on. Very few questionnaires exclusively use 'open-ended' questions in which people are invited to write down without limit what they feel about a particular issue. Most questionnaires tend to use a combination of closed questions with tick-boxes or attitudinal scales (e.g. on a scale of 1–5, 1 being strongly agree and 5 being strongly disagree), with some occasional open-ended questions.

Strengths of questionnaires

Questionnaires have various strengths:

- First, questionnaires are useful for researching large numbers of people because they are reasonably cheap to design, print, distribute and analyse compared with other methods.
- Second, if an effective sampling frame exists, they can be sent through the post and therefore distributed to a geographically dispersed sample that can be compared for regional variations in behaviour and attitude.
- Third, postal questionnaires are more likely to generate representative samples because they can be sent out to thousands of people.
- Fourth, questionnaires are customer-friendly in that they involve less time and effort for the research subject compared with other methods as it does not take long to complete a set of closed questions.
- Fifth, questionnaires involve the minimum of contact with research subjects. The researcher is unlikely to be present when the respondent fills in the questionnaire and therefore is unlikely to influence the results.
- Sixth, questionnaires may be useful for research into embarrassing, sensitive or deviant behaviour, especially if the researcher guarantees both anonymity and confidentiality. Moreover, people may prefer to answer questions on such topics in the privacy of their own homes rather than face to face with an interviewer.
- Finally, according to positivist sociologists, questionnaires have the theoretical advantage of having the following scientific characteristics: a well-designed questionnaire will be high in reliability, objective and value-free, and will produce lots of quantitative data that can be compared and correlated. Moreover, such data should be highly valid. If everyone is answering exactly the same questions, they are responding to the same thing. Thus any difference in the answers should reflect differences in real life.

Weaknesses of questionnaires

A number of potential practical and theoretical problems have been identified with the questionnaire, especially the postal version.

- The biggest practical problem is persuading people to return the questionnaire. This is less of a problem for those given out by hand because it is likely that the researcher will be waiting nearby to collect them in. However, it is a huge problem for postal questionnaires, which consequently suffer from very poor response rates or returns. If a response rate dips below 50%, this is likely to undermine the representativeness of the group being researched. Furthermore, those who have

Exam tip

Aim to give examples of loaded and leading questions.

Exam tip

It is important that you are able to identify theoretical as well as practical and ethical reasons why a sociologist uses a method like questionnaires or interviews. Ask yourself why might a positivist or interpretivist like or dislike this method. If you do this well, it should push your response into the top band of the marking scheme.

responded may be biased in that they are more likely to have a special interest in whatever is being researched.

■ Another practical problem of questionnaires and the quantitative data that they generate is that a questionnaire is one-dimensional in its emphasis on closed questions. These may give sociologists information about patterns and trends but it is difficult to go into any depth about motives or reasons for behaviour in a questionnaire because they need to be kept short and simple. As a result, researchers can never be sure that all respondents have interpreted the questions in the same way (although a pilot survey will hopefully minimise this possibility). Some respondents may not cooperate with the research because they feel frustrated as the research design does not allow them to elaborate on their feelings and emotions.

Interpretivist sociologists criticise the use of questionnaires because they believe people interpret them in ways that undermine the validity of the data they collect. For example, they argue that some people (especially those engaged in immoral, deviant or criminal behaviour) may associate questionnaires with authority (regardless of guarantees of anonymity) and consequently may be less likely to respond to them, or if they do they may be less likely to give truthful responses because they feel threatened. Similarly, people like to engage in 'positive impression management'. This means that questions about socially approved or respectable behaviour such as charitable actions are disproportionately more likely to be answered in the affirmative. Likewise, people disproportionately respond in the negative with regard to questions that ask about behaviour that others morally judge and disapprove of. Others (especially young males) may interpret questionnaires as an opportunity to show off by exaggerating their behaviour.

Another problem relating to questionnaires that interpretivists have highlighted is the 'imposition problem'. They point out that questionnaires are designed and the data they collect is analysed by professional sociologists. However, it is extremely unlikely that such sociologists have had much contact with the research group or have had any real insight before beginning their research into how members of the research group interpret their social reality. Consequently, questionnaire design tends to reflect those factors that the sociologist thinks are important.

In contrast, the research subjects may believe other factors (not considered by the sociologist) are more important but are unable to state this because the questions have simply not been asked. Similarly, when the researchers interpret the data collected by the questionnaire, they may apply a different meaning to that actually intended by those filling in the questionnaire. Interpretivists are therefore critical of questionnaires because they lack the means of looking inside people's heads — this is known as verstehen — and truly understanding their social reality.

Structured interviews

A structured interview involves the researcher reading out questions from a questionnaire known as an interview schedule and writing down the respondent's answers. Such interviews allow little flexibility, that is, the interviewer is not normally allowed to deviate from the questions on the interview schedule. Such interviews are very popular with market researchers. The data collected is usually expressed in quantitative form.

Strengths of structured interviews

Many of the strengths of the structured interview are much the same as those of the questionnaire because the interview schedule is also a questionnaire that mainly uses closed questions using fixed category answers and tick-boxes — the only real difference is that the interviewer reads it out and fills it in on behalf of the interviewee. Positivist sociologists therefore are keen on this research tool because like the questionnaire, it has the scientific characteristics of reliability, objectivity and quantifiability.

Structured interviews can be carried out on relatively large samples because they can be conducted fairly quickly. They normally take anything between 10 and 30 minutes each to complete. However, the structured interview does have some advantages over the questionnaire, especially the postal version.

- First, interviewers can ensure that the right person is answering the questions, which is nigh on impossible for researchers using the postal questionnaire.
- Second, interviewers can explain the aims and objectives and make sure the respondent is happy to participate. This may reduce potential non-response.
- Third, structured interviews have better response rates than postal questionnaires because the interviewer can call back if a potential respondent is not at home.
- Fourth, an interviewee can ask for clarification of questions they do not understand (although such questions should have been weeded out at the pilot interview stage).
- Finally, the interviewer can add to the quality of the survey data by observing the social context of responses, e.g. the facial expression, tone of voice, body language, attitude etc. of the respondent. The interviewer can also record information about the respondent, where they live, their social status and so on.

Weaknesses of structured interviews

The structured interview experiences some of the same problems as the questionnaire because the interview schedule has been designed in much the same way. Structured interviews, like questionnaires, are artificial devices which are not a normal part of everyday reality.

Interpretivists also note the impact of the more general problem of 'interview bias', which takes four potential forms.

1 Interviewees may react negatively to the social characteristics of the interviewer — their gender, ethnicity, age, perceived authority, accent and so on — and may not cooperate, or if they do they may engage in deception because they are anxious that the data might be used against them in some way.

2 There may be a 'social desirability' effect caused by 'demand characteristics' — this refers to the situation in which respondents work out from the research design what the researcher is looking for or they defer to interviewers and are eager to please them. The result of such interpretations is that interviewees may subconsciously change their behaviour to fit in with the research aims and give the researchers the replies they think the sociologist wants to hear.

3 The problems of 'impression management' and 'imposition' discussed as disadvantages of the questionnaire method above are also associated with the structured interview.

Knowledge check 13

Why does the structured interview share many of the strengths of the survey questionnaire?

4   There is a danger that interviewers may unconsciously lead respondents into particular biased responses through their tone of voice or by their facial expression or body language.

Interpretivists are also critical of structured interviews for much the same theoretical reasons that they are of questionnaires. They argue that the questions asked during such interviews are likely to be superficial and they fail to achieve verstehen — to achieve the sorts of qualitative data needed to understand how and why people interpret the world around them and behave the way they do.

Interpretivists highlight the inflexibility of the structured interview. The robotic adherence to the interview schedule means that researchers rarely follow up interesting responses or ask why people behave in the way they do. Researchers do not have the time to build up the trust and rapport required to generate truly authentic data. Moreover, interpretivist sociologists point out that there is often a gap between what people say they do and what they actually do in practice. Many people are unaware that they behave in the way they do. Interpretivist sociologists argue that these types of behaviour can be uncovered only through the use of methods such as participant observation.

Knowledge check 14
Why is the structured interview often an inflexible method of collecting information?

Statistical data (official and non-official)

Official statistics

Official statistics are produced by government departments. They tend to come from two broad sources. First, the Office for National Statistics (ONS) gathers statistics that cover all aspects of economic and social life, such as productivity, work, consumption of consumer goods, unemployment, crime, births, deaths, marriage, divorce, health, family life, education and so on. In this way it uncovers patterns and trends in the economic and social performance of the UK as a whole (compared with other nations), to measure how effective government departments and institutions such as the NHS are and to map out the life-chances of the UK population according to social class, gender, age, disability, ethnicity and so on.

Second, the government employs social researchers to survey particular populations, usually to work out the efficacy of certain social policies. Every 10 years, the government carries out a mass questionnaire survey aimed at every household in the UK. This is called the census, which aims, in the words of the ONS, to 'help paint a picture of the nation and how we live'. It provides a detailed snapshot of the population and its characteristics so that funding can be applied more effectively to public services. The last census was carried out in 2011.

Non-official statistics

These are the product of agencies outside of the government. For example, businesses, trade unions, political parties, pressure groups, think-tanks, research organisations such as the Joseph Rowntree Foundation or the Sutton Trust, the mass media and so on carry out research which results in statistical data relating to most aspects of social life.

Strengths of official and non-official statistics

Official statistics are extremely easy and very cheap to access — they are often available via the internet and access to them therefore involves little effort or cost for the sociologist. Moreover, they are often very up to date. This means that they also have a useful comparative value in that past statistical trends and patterns can be compared with the present in order to assess the success or failure of social policies and/or the performance of particular social groups or agencies such as the educational system. For example, by examining statistics over a period of time, sociologists can work out whether the distribution of wealth and poverty has widened or narrowed over the past 100 years. Both official and non-official statistics are useful because they help to identify correlations between social phenomena. For example, by examining groups of statistics, sociologists might see a relationship between poverty, ethnicity and mortality.

Positivist sociologists generally tend to be keen on using official statistics because they believe this data is collected in a scientific way, that is, in a standardised, reliable and objective fashion. Government surveys also tend to use large representative and often national samples and therefore their findings can usually be generalised to similar populations. The census, of course, surveys the whole of the British population rather than a sample of it.

Weaknesses of official and non-official statistics

Both official and non-official statistics can be problematic in terms of their use by sociologists, for several reasons. First, such statistics are not collected for sociological purposes. This may limit their usefulness and validity because the definitions and concepts used by the government or non-official agencies may differ from those preferred by sociologists. For example, the definition of poverty used by the government or a right-wing think-tank may differ considerably from that used by those sociologists who believe that poverty is a massive social problem. One reason for this is that official and non-official agencies may not be as objective as positivist sociologists paint them out to be. They often have a political agenda and consequently various biases may underpin any statistical data they produce. For example, a government may manipulate or massage statistics on unemployment, poverty and inequality in order to manage the electorate's impression of its policies as effective. Consequently, such statistics may not present a complete picture of what is going on.

Interpretivist sociologists tend to be sceptical about the value of both official and non-official statistics because they point out that such statistics are socially constructed. This means that they don't just appear or happen. Rather, they are the social product or end result of a powerful social group making a decision or judgement that a particular set of activities needs recording and that statistics need collecting. However, these decisions are sometimes selective and biased and consequently the statistics may say more about the powerful group that does the collecting than the social phenomena they are supposedly documenting or measuring. For example, the fact that black people are disproportionately represented in the official criminal statistics may be the product of police behaviour rather than black people being more criminal than other social groups. Interpretivists also argue that official and non-official statistics give little insight into the human stories behind them. For example, unemployment statistics do not tell sociologists anything about the everyday experience and humiliation of being unemployed.

Knowledge check 15

Why do interpretivists claim that official statistics are socially constructed and therefore biased?

Content analysis

Content analysis is a quantitative research method, which is mainly used by sociologists to analyse mass media products such as advertisements, magazines, newspapers, television news reports and even children's books and fairy tales. It involves counting the frequency of certain images such as those contained in adverts and photographs or words contained in newspaper/magazine articles or headlines. A study of a link between media and anorexia, for example, might involve the sociologist counting the number of times images of ultra-thin models appear in magazines aimed at young females.

Content analysis is normally based on a researcher constructing a content analysis schedule — this is a set of categories related to, for example, images and/or text that the researcher believes operationalises a research question or hypothesis. The researcher then samples the mass media product they are interested in and uses the content analysis schedule to 'observe', count and record how often the image and/or text occurs.

Content analysis is generally regarded as a cheap and easily accessible means of research because mass media reports are readily available.

Content analysis also allows the sociologist to compare mass media products or content over a period of time. In other words, both content analysis and semiotics can be longitudinal, for example, advertisements or the content of children's books can be analysed from different time periods to work out whether their patriarchal content is increasing or decreasing. Finally, positivist sociologists regard content analysis as reliable because other sociologists can easily repeat and cross-check the results.

However, content analysis has been criticised because counting media images or particular uses of text tells sociologists next to nothing about how those who use the media interpret or are affected by this content; it is just assumed that they do. At best, it can be argued that these images and text only give insight into the values and prejudices of those responsible for the social construction of media products, that is, journalists, editors, broadcasters, advertising executives and so on.

Ethnography

'Ethnography' refers to any qualitative research project that is focused on providing a detailed and in-depth description of the everyday lives and practices of a group of people that is as faithful as possible to the way those people see their lives themselves. Such a group may be large, as in the case of community studies of whole towns, or quite small, for example, there are ethnographic studies of delinquent young males ('Street Corner Society' by Bill Whyte or 'A View from the Boys' by Howard Parker), gangs ('Gang Leader for a Day' by Sudhir Venkatesh), groups of school pupils, or people in institutions such as mental hospitals.

Ethnography is normally the preserve of interpretivist sociology, which believes that researchers should focus on how people interact socially and how they interpret and socially construct their social reality. Interpretivist sociologists are very keen to 'get inside the heads of the people they are studying' so that they can see the world through their eyes. The main idea underpinning ethnography therefore is to get an insider's point of view and to 'tell it like it is' rather than to seek causes and

> **Exam tip**
>
> Note that content analysis is an unusual method because it combines the use of both primary and secondary data. The secondary data take the form of media reports that are analysed by the sociologist, therefore producing primary data.

explanations, which are generally the main motives of positivist survey-style research. This is not to say that interpretivist research does not begin with a hypothesis; it is just that interpretivists are happy to let hypotheses emerge from the research as it develops and progresses rather than imposing previous sociological models or experiences on the research.

Ethnographic research often means long-term involvement in the everyday setting in which the research subjects are active. This may mean spending many months or even years in the places where the research subjects are to be found. The most common type of ethnographic research method is participant observation, which aims to develop an understanding of what it is like to live in a particular setting and to participate in the daily life of those being studied while observing it. Another type of ethnographic research is the unstructured or informal interview. Such interviews are often part and parcel of the observation process, for example, a participant observer is likely to engage those being observed in conversation in order to validate what the observer thinks is happening. However, unstructured interviews are often adopted by interpretivist sociologists as a method in their own right. They are normally carried out in a natural setting that the interviewee finds comfortable, such as their home.

Unstructured interviews

An unstructured interview is like a guided conversation, in that the interaction and talk between the sociologist and the interviewee are informal but the researcher plays an active yet subtle role in managing questions about the research topic to ensure that the interviewee remains focused on it. The emphasis in these types of open-ended interviews is on spontaneity, flexibility and building trust. A successful unstructured interview is likely to be one in which the interviewee feels relaxed and unthreatened because the situation in which the questions are being asked feels natural. A skilled interviewer expertly and flexibly probes and follows up responses in such a sympathetic and empathetic way that the interviewee feels that a bond or rapport has been established and they trust the interviewer so much that they are willing to volunteer richly detailed and qualitative information that they would not normally offer up in more formal research contexts.

> **Exam tip**
>
> Remember to stress that interpretivists prefer these types of interviews, in contrast with structured interviews, which positivists are more likely to employ.

Interpretivist sociologists are keen on this method for four main reasons:

1 The style of these types of interview is likely to put the interviewee at ease, which means they are more likely to open up and say what they really feel and mean. In this sense, this type of interview is more likely to achieve verstehen, that is, to authentically see the world from the point of view of those being researched.

2 The emphasis in these types of interviews is to make the interviewee the centre of the research because if the subjects of the research can see that the researchers are genuinely interested in their experiences or are sympathetic to their situation, then they will be more willing to divulge and discuss sensitive issues and/or painful experiences that are unlikely to be revealed under other circumstances.

3 This unique and original material can lead to the development of fresh and novel hypotheses, which can be tested as the interviews progress.

4 The spontaneity, flexibility and trust generated by such interviews mean that they produce highly valid data of first-hand accounts and interpretations of the issue that is being studied, often in the everyday speech of those being interviewed.

Positivist sociologists are highly critical of unstructured interviews, however, because they allegedly are unscientific in that they lack reliability and objectivity. Positivists claim that they cannot be replicated because they are the product of the unique relationship that has been established between the interviewer and the interviewee. A different interviewer is therefore unlikely to achieve the same or similar results. Moreover, there is no standardised interview schedule that another sociologist could adopt to help repeat the research. Positivists also claim that such interviews and the data they generate are biased by the interviewers becoming too emotionally close to their interviewees and losing their objective detachment and neutrality.

Positivists note that unstructured interviews are problematic for a number of practical reasons:

■ They are often exceptionally time-consuming and therefore expensive to conduct and transcribe.
■ They are also costly because the interviewing team's training needs to be thorough and specialised, for example, interviewers need to be trained in interpersonal skills in order to establish positive relationships with their interviewees.
■ This type of research may involve a series of trust-building interviews with just one interviewee. However, the time-consuming nature of this method means that the number of those who participate as interviewees is likely to be smaller than the number of those found in survey-type research, which means that it is less likely to be representative of the population the sociologist is interested in.
■ Finally, the qualitative nature of the data collected is not easily converted into a form that can be analysed, categorised, compared and correlated.

Semi-structured interviews

Semi-structured interviews are made up of a combination of closed questions, aimed at eliciting factual information about the respondent, and open questions, which are usually aimed at obtaining information about people's motivations, feelings etc. For example, closed questions might ask about age, occupation (in order to work out social class), gender and ethnicity as well as posing questions with fixed-choice response tick-boxes, which are then followed by open questions asking 'why' or 'how' the person chose the response they did.

Semi-structured interviews, therefore, allow the interviewer to ask respondents for clarification of vague answers and to follow up and develop their responses. For example, the interviewer can jog a respondent's memory and ask them to give examples. These and other techniques can add depth and detail to responses, and can help the sociologist to assess the participant's truthfulness. However, the reliability of such interviews has been called into question because an interviewer might find that some interviewees need more probing than others. This may mean that every interview is different, so the data may not be strictly comparable as to some extent the interviewees may be responding to different questions.

Observations

There are broadly three types of observation:

1 External (also known as direct or remote) observation.
2 Overt participant observation, which involves a group agreeing to let a sociologist take part in their everyday activities, usually for a fairly long period of time.

Exam tip

Be able to compare the advantages/ weaknesses of the three different types of interviews. Think too about variations on interviews, such as group interviews and focus groups.

3   Covert participant observation, which involves the researcher taking an undercover role, infiltrating a group who have no knowledge that he or she is a sociologist and interacting with that group as a peer.

Non-participant observation

External or direct observation involves a non-participant observer simply watching and recording interaction and behaviour in a given situation such as a classroom or public place. Such an observer may be openly observing, for example, the presence of a stranger in a classroom will alert students to an observation, or discreet, for example, the observer may be sitting in a café or bar but be recording people's behaviour without their knowledge. Some researchers may choose to observe a group or interaction via a CCTV camera or one-way mirror. Direct observation normally involves the observer using an observation schedule made up of a set of categories of behaviour that they might be expected to see that can be ticked off and quantified. The existence of an observation schedule means that this research method is reasonably reliable as it can be repeated by other researchers.

Supporters of this type of observation argue that because the researcher is detached and therefore objective, their interpretation of the group's behaviour is less likely to be biased. Moreover, because the researcher does not make any decisions or join in the group's activities, the group itself will not be influenced by the observer. However, this is a contentious point. Critics of non-participant observation point out that if the observer is visible then those being observed are likely to act unnaturally because they may feel anxious or threatened by the fact that the observation is taking place. If the observation is not supported by other methods such as interviews it is unlikely to provide much insight into why people behave in the way that they do.

Participant observation: overt and covert

Overt participant observation

Participant observation involves the observer immersing themselves in the lifestyle of the group being studied 24 hours per day for months or even years. These sociologists participate in the same activities as the group being researched and observe their everyday lives. The aim is to understand what is happening from the point of view of those involved; to 'get inside their heads' and to understand the meaning that they ascribe to their situation.

Usually, the observer gains access to the group via a gate-keeper — someone who belongs to the group and who has the respect and trust of the others and is therefore able to gain their consent. Sometimes the researcher can access a group by offering a service such as legal advice (e.g. Elliot Liebow's 'Tally's Corner') or acting as a lookout (e.g. Laud Humphreys' 'Tearoom Trade'), by cultivating friendships (Howard Parker's 'A View from the Boys') or by having certain skills (Howard Becker's 'Outsiders') and so on.

This type of observation is usually supplemented with informal or unstructured interviews, that is, conversations that take place during the course of the observation. The observer will use these to cross-check with members of the group that what they are observing is shared by all members of the group, so increasing the validity of the data. However, data gathering should begin only when the observer is sure that the early disruption to the natural behaviour of the group caused by their participation has dissipated and the group has returned to its natural routine. Participant observation involves 'hanging around' waiting for something to happen — in this sense, it is often misinterpreted and criticised as unstructured and unplanned. However, this is because the interpretivist sociologists who carry out this type of research generally go into it open-minded. They are willing to let their hypotheses and research aims develop organically as the research progresses because observation and conversation often eventually result in the observer learning the answers to questions they would not normally have asked if using questionnaires and interviews.

Covert participant observation

Sometimes it is impossible to find a gate-keeper or the group is just not interested in being the subject of research because they are engaged in illegal and/or deviant activities or are suspicious of conventional society, such as might be found with religious sects. Sometimes the researcher might simply believe that overt research is too likely to produce artificial behaviour in those being observed, especially if it is a group that is accountable, such as the police. In order to overcome these sorts of problems a researcher might decide to infiltrate the group covertly by taking on a different identity.

This type of undercover observation takes considerable skill (and often courage) if it is to be successful because the person under cover needs to be a convincing actor and has to be constantly on guard against their cover being blown. They must find a way of recording information that is not going to arouse suspicion. Such research is very stressful because it involves constant vigilance in order not to lose the trust and confidence of the group, constant risk-taking and even physical danger.

Strengths of participant observation

Interpretivist sociologists are very keen on this method because it achieves verstehen — the researcher sees things through the eyes of the group being studied because they are in the same situation as the group's members and they experience what the members of the group are experiencing. The sociologist therefore gains a first-hand insider's view through watching and listening, and uncovers the priorities, concerns, anxieties and motivations of the observed group as they actually unfurl. The sociological observer will probably see things that are unlikely to be voluntarily revealed in an interview or on a questionnaire.

Observation is high in validity because the researcher can see what people do in their natural setting as opposed to what they say they do when asked in questionnaires or interviews. Authenticity is therefore paramount, especially if using covert observation, because the observed behaviour is natural. Those being observed are less likely to be influenced by the artificiality of a research situation, which may produce responses shaped by demand characteristics, impression management and so on.

Observation can often lead to unexpected findings that generate new hypotheses and insights into people's behaviour. A skilled, open-minded observer avoids the imposition problem and should be able to validate their observations by supplementing these with conversations with members of the group. Additionally, observers often engage in reflexivity and record all their interactions in a research diary to assess whether the behaviour they observe is the result of their presence.

Exam tip

The examiner may ask about the merits of covert forms of observation compared with participant observation.

Participant observation is longitudinal and therefore allows an understanding of how changes in attitudes and behaviour take place over months and years. Methods such as questionnaires and interviews can give only a snapshot picture, that is, how people felt at the moment they filled in the questionnaire or took part in the interview.

Weaknesses of participant observation

Most of the critique of participant observation comes from the positivist tradition.

- Positivists believe that participant observation breaks a number of ethical rules. Covert observation has especially been criticised for its deception. It is argued that it abuses the trust and friendship of people in the group who are being observed. However, Humphreys has defended the use of covert observation by pointing out that the groups being observed are unlikely to normally cooperate with and give consent to sociological research. Moreover, the results gained from such research outweigh the ethical concerns because they are truly authentic and are untainted by both researcher imposition and the suspicions and anxieties that other forms of sociological research might produce in research populations. Participant observation has also been criticised because some observers have taken part in illegal or unethical behaviour in order to gain or reinforce the trust of the group being researched.

- Participant observation has been accused of not being objective. It is suggested that observers are often biased because they become too sympathetic towards those they are observing. It is claimed that it is too easy for observers to lose their detachment and 'go native'. The observer then interprets the behaviour of the group in a positive light, which allegedly biases their analysis of the group's actions.

- Critics stress the unreliability of participant observation. There is no way that the research can be repeated as a means of verifying its descriptions and conclusions. It is not possible to judge whether the social context or the people studied are representative, or whether the presence of the researcher changed the behaviour of the group more than was realised. Moreover, the success of the research is often due to the exclusive relationships they have constructed. Another sociologist might find it impossible to gain the same degree of trust and rapport with the observed group.

- This type of research is criticised for being unrepresentative because the observer cannot practically study large numbers of people or the wider context within which the research setting is located.

- Participant observation has a number of practical problems. It is very time-consuming and expensive.

Exam tip

Be specific when answering questions on observation, as there are different types.

Mixed methods

Most sociologists use a combination of research techniques as well as both quantitative and qualitative data rather than confining themselves to one method. There are two approaches to mixing methods.

Triangulation

Triangulation is usually adopted so that the sociologist is able to get a better view of the overall picture of what they are studying by looking at it from a number of different angles. It normally involves combining methods that result in quantitative and qualitative data in order to check and verify the validity and reliability of the data collected by each method. For example, a sociologist using participant observation might check the validity of their findings by asking the research subject(s) to take part in unstructured interviews which ask how the interviewees interpreted a situation observed by the sociologist in order to make sure that the sociologist fully understood what was going on. The sociologist might also ask subjects to keep a diary of their actions, which can be compared with their own observations in order to validate them. Qualitative research may also produce hypotheses that can be checked using statistical methods, for example, participant observation might produce unexpected behaviour that could be further investigated using a questionnaire survey.

Methodological pluralism

Methodological pluralism combines research methods in order to build up a fuller picture of what is being studied. For example, a researcher might begin their research by looking at official statistics relating to the behaviour they are investigating. They might then proceed to conduct a social survey questionnaire using large samples of people scattered across the country in order to test whether the behavioural trends seen in the official statistics have changed. Finally, in order to elicit qualitative data about why people behave in the way they do, a small sample of people might be invited to take part in in-depth unstructured interviews.

> **Exam tip**
>
> Make sure you know the sociological justification for using triangulation rather than methodological pluralism.

Problems with using mixed methods

Three problems have been identified with the use of mixed methods:

1. They are often expensive and produce vast amounts of data, which can be difficult to analyse.

2. Priority tends to be given to one method at the expense of the others — they rarely have equal status. This is because survey researchers do not have the same skills as ethnographers and vice versa.

3. Mixed methods can sometimes produce contradictory findings. This poses a problem in terms of what should be kept and what should be discarded.

Summary

- Questionnaire surveys are probably the most popular research method used by sociologists, but despite their advantage in hitting large numbers of people, they can be one-dimensional and superficial in terms of the data collected.
- Structured interviews also gather large amounts of data, but the validity of this data can be undermined by the interaction between the interviewer and the interviewee.
- A cheap source of data is that collected by official agencies, such as government departments, although sociologists need to be careful when using this data because it is not collected for sociological reasons.
- Some sociologists prefer to immerse themselves in the everyday lives of those being studied in order to produce data high in validity and therefore adopt ethnographic methods such as unstructured interviews and participant observation, which involves establishing trusting and qualitative relationships with those being studied.
- Most participant observation is carried out with the knowledge of the group being observed, but some is covert and consequently is considered by some positivist sociologists to be unethical.
- Most sociologists use a mixture of methods in order to generate both quantitative and qualitative data.

■ Section B Understanding social inequalities

What are the main patterns and trends in social inequality and difference?

Social inequality and social class

The opportunity for members of the working class to experience upward social mobility is hindered by factors such as low income, lack of access to wealth, poverty, the experience of education and so on.

Income

The UK has a very high level of income inequality compared with that of other developed countries. In particular, between 1979 and 1997 income inequality between the rich and poor widened until it was at its greatest since records began at the end of the nineteenth century. Between 1979 and 1992, average income rose by 36%, but it rose by 62% for the top 10% of earners, while it fell by 17% for the poorest 10% of earners. According to the Equality Trust in 2015, people in the bottom 10% of the population have on average a net income of £8,468, while the top 10% have net incomes almost ten times that (£79,042). However, there are also great variations in the top 10%. In 2012, the top 1% had an average income of £259,917, while the top 0.1% had an average income of £941,582. Overall, the richest 20% of society have 40% of income, while the poorest 20% have only 8% of income.

The Low Pay Unit argues that low pay is the most important cause of poverty in the UK. About 45% of British workers are earning less than two-thirds of the average hourly wage. Wilkinson and Pickett found that poverty brings with it various socioeconomic disadvantages, including debt, poor diet, weak immune systems and therefore higher levels of illness and disability, lower life expectancy, high divorce rates, low educational achievement, poor housing, depression and a disproportionate number of suicides.

Wealth

In 2014, the richest 1% of the population owned as much wealth as the poorest 55% according to the ONS. In 2014, Oxfam reported that five billionaire families controlled the same wealth as 20% of the population, or 12 million people.

Education

At all stages of education, students from working-class backgrounds achieve less than their middle-class counterparts. Even when working-class children have the same level of intelligence as middle-class children they are:

- less likely to attend nursery schools or preschool playgroups
- more likely to start school unable to read
- more likely to fall behind their middle-class peers in reading, writing and maths
- more likely to be placed in lower sets or streams.

Exam tip

There is no need to know statistics by heart but you should have a good idea of trends and patterns.

Knowledge check 16

What is the difference between wealth and income?

In 2015, the Sutton Trust reported that more than one-third (36%) of bright but disadvantaged boys and just under a quarter (24%) of clever but poor girls seriously underachieve at GCSE. These figures compare with only 16% of boys and 9% of girls from better-off homes. The Sutton Trust also pointed out in 2015 that despite the fact that only 7% of the school population is privately educated, more than 50% of the Cabinet and over a third of MPs are privately educated. Sutton Trust research has also indicated that privately educated graduates get bigger pay rises than their state school peers.

Knowledge check 17

Why do only 7% of pupils attend private schools?

Social mobility

In 2015, both official government statistics and a report by the Organisation for Economic Co-operation and Development (OECD) on social mobility across the globe concluded that Britain has some of the lowest social mobility in the developed world. Moreover, social mobility in the UK has got worse since the 1970s. For example, the number of people from poor families going to university in 2015 has fallen compared with the 1990s, while the number of graduates from better-off homes has increased. Moreover, only 3% of the richest fifth in society have mothers with no qualifications compared with 46% of the poorest fifth. Only 49% of the poorest who apply for university get in compared with 77% of the richest.

Evidence also suggests that parental influences, as well as the connections made in private schools, are more important in shaping a child's future than the qualifications they gain or the quality of their schooling. The OECD research concludes that there is a strong link between a lack of social mobility and inequality — and the UK has both. Only Portugal is more unequal, with less social mobility.

Exam tip

It can be useful to know how the UK compares with social inequaities in other parts of the world.

Health

Working-class people experience poorer mortality and morbidity rates than the middle class. Over 3,500 more working-class babies would survive per year if the working-class infant mortality rate was reduced to middle-class levels. Wilkinson and Pickett found that working-class people are more likely to die before retirement of cancer, stroke and heart disease than middle-class people. In London, there is a 25-year life expectancy gap between the rich and the poor.

Social inequality and gender

The opportunity for females to experience upward social mobility is made more difficult by factors such as horizontal and vertical segregation in the workplace, poverty, poor health, educational choices and so on.

Work and employment: horizontal segregation

The UK labour market is characterised by horizontal segregation, meaning that different sectors of employment are dominated by either male or female workers. For example, women make up about 79% of the health and social work workforce whereas in the private sector women are over-concentrated in clerical, administrative, retail and personal services, such as catering, while men are mainly found in the skilled manual and upper professional sectors (Equal Opportunities Commission (EOC),

2006). Men are ten times more likely than women to be employed in skilled trades and are also more likely to be managers and senior officials. Men are more likely to be self-employed than women.

Work and employment: vertical segregation

The UK labour market is also characterised by vertical segregation, meaning that males and females dominate different levels of jobs in terms of status, skill and pay. The evidence suggests that within occupational groups, women tend to be concentrated at the lower levels. When women do gain access to the upper professional or management sector, the evidence suggests that they encounter a 'glass ceiling' — they can see the top jobs but restrictions or discrimination create barriers that prevent women getting into them. The Equality and Human Rights Commission noted in 2008 that women in the UK lack access to the most powerful jobs and that it will take 55 years at the current rate of progress for women to achieve equal status with men at senior levels in the judiciary and 73 years for equality to be achieved in senior management jobs in Britain's top 100 companies.

A gender pay gap also exists. According to the feminist research centre the Fawcett Society, the pay gap between men and women in 2014 stood at 19% measured by gross hourly pay. The Society argues that this gap is caused by a 'motherhood penalty' (that is, motherhood often results in part-time work), vertical segregation, which means that women are disproportionately employed in temporary and casual labour, and outright discrimination by employers.

Poverty

Some sociologists claim that inequalities in employment mean there has been a 'feminisation of poverty' because women generally do not earn as much as men as they are likely to be in low-status, low-skilled and part-time work. Moreover, women are often unable to work because they are full-time carers of children, the sick and disabled, and the elderly. Older women are more likely to be in poverty compared with elderly men because they may have spent substantial periods of their lives in the home as mothers and housewives, and therefore they are less likely to have an occupational pension.

Health

Graham points out that women have higher rates of illness than men, especially in terms of chronic long-term sickness, disability and mental illness. Bernard suggests that marriage makes women sick because evidence suggests that married women experience worse health than married men and single women. Women may experience greater stress than men because they are likely to care for both children and other relatives, i.e. ageing parents.

Education

Feminists have pointed out that, despite the fact that girls' achievements in education outstrip those of males, the 'hidden curriculum' means that subject choices in secondary schools and in further and higher education still tend to be gender-stereotyped. This leads to the reinforcement of vertical gender segregation in the workplace because choice of degree subjects is likely to influence career and therefore opportunities for upward social mobility.

Knowledge check 18

Which group applies the motherhood penalty to women workers according to feminists?

Social inequality and ethnicity

The opportunity for members of ethnic minority groups to experience upward social mobility is made more difficult by factors such as discrimination in the workplace, disproportionate unemployment rates, poverty and so on.

Employment

Ethnic-minority men are over-represented in the low-skilled, low-paid and insecure service sector, particularly in the restaurant and retail industries. One in eight taxi drivers in the UK come from Pakistani backgrounds. In contrast, very few ethnic minorities are engaged in white-collar, professional or managerial work, although people from Indian and Chinese backgrounds are more likely than other ethnic minority groups to be found in middle-class non-manual occupations such as accountancy, law and medicine. For example, approximately 1 in 20 working Indian men is a medical practitioner — almost ten times the national average.

Between 2012 and 2014 unemployment levels for the UK as a whole and for white ethnic groups remained constant — at 8% and 7% respectively. However, unemployment among ethnic minority groups rose from 13% to 14%. Unemployment among black ethnic minorities rose from 16% to 17%, while it rose from 17% to 19% for Pakistani/Bangladeshi ethnic groups. In 2014, 16–24-year-olds from ethnic minority backgrounds had an unemployment rate of 37%, up from 33% in 2012. In contrast, unemployment in this age group in general across the whole of the UK was 21% during 2011–14.

Research has also found that African-Caribbean graduates are twice as likely to be unemployed than white graduates, while African men with degrees are seven times more likely to be unemployed than white male graduates.

In 2009, researchers from the National Centre for Social Research sent out nearly 3,000 job applications under false identities using the surnames of Mahmood, Namagembe and Taylor. Each application had a similar level of work experience, a British education, a good set of qualifications and excellent work histories. The researchers found that the Taylor identity sent out on average nine applications before receiving an invitation for an interview while the Mahmood and Namagembe identities had to send out an average of 16 applications before they received a positive response.

Income

In 2004, the Ethnic Minorities Employment Task Force reported that ethnic minorities generally earn lower incomes than white people, on average £7,000 less per year. Research by the Joseph Rowntree Foundation in 2007 found that men from ethnic minorities in managerial and professional jobs earn up to 25% less than their white colleagues. The Labour Force Survey of 2011–13 found that in London 44% of Bangladeshis and Pakistani employees were paid below the living wage compared with only 20% of white employees. Research by Longhi suggests these striking differences in wages between the white majority and ethnic and religious groups persist, and that Pakistani Muslims are the ethnic-religious group likely to be receiving the lowest incomes.

Knowledge check 19

Why do you think one in seven taxi drivers in the UK come from either Pakistani or Bangladeshi social backgrounds?

Knowledge check 20

What does this experiment generally suggest about employers?

Poverty

Research by the Joseph Rowntree Foundation in 2007 showed that 40% of ethnic minority communities in the UK live in poverty — double the poverty rates of white communities. Half of all ethnic minority children in the UK live in poverty. In 2015, Fisher and Nandi's research concluded that Pakistani and Bangladeshi groups, followed by black African and black Caribbean groups, were the groups most likely to be found in persistent poverty. They found that 37% of Pakistanis were in poverty for two consecutive years and 14% in poverty for three consecutive years. Only a third (32%) of Pakistanis and Bangladeshis did not experience poverty in the period 2009 to 2012.

Alcock identifies a range of different forms of poverty and exclusion that ethnic minorities in the UK experience, which has a significant negative effect on the chances of ethnic minorities to experience upward social mobility. Alcock observes that 70% of all people from ethnic minorities live in the 88 most deprived local authority districts compared with only 40% of the general population, and generally live in poor quality and overcrowded housing.

Health

In 2013, the Joseph Rowntree Foundation reported that persistent inequalities could be seen in the health of Pakistani and Bangladeshi women whose illness rates have been 10% higher than those of white women in 1991, 2001 and 2011. Surveys show that Pakistani, Bangladeshi and black Caribbean people report the poorest health, with Indian, East African, Asian and black African people reporting the same health as white British people. It was also reported in 2008 that the infant mortality rate of babies from Pakistani and Caribbean communities born in 2005 was twice as high as that among white babies.

Education

Chinese and Indian pupils do very well in school, but the evidence suggests that Pakistani and black Caribbean young people still have lower GCSE attainment levels than most other ethnic groups, although these have significantly improved since 2007. More than half of children from Asian households are eligible for free school meals (a sign of family poverty). Children who are eligible for free school meals are far less likely to achieve expected outcomes for Key Stages 1–4. African-Caribbean boys are three times more likely to be permanently excluded from school than white pupils.

> **Exam tip**
>
> Try to avoid careless language when describing ethnic minorities. For example, 'ethnics' is not an acceptable term.

Social inequality and age

Age intersects with other structural influences such as class, gender and ethnicity and results in inequalities experienced by both the elderly and the young.

The elderly

Bradley refers to age as the neglected dimension of inequality. In pre-industrial societies, the elderly have status and influence, but in industrial societies, the elderly are seen as lacking the ability to contribute meaningfully and are often excluded from full involvement in society. This social exclusion has two major effects.

Poverty

According to the ONS, about 16% of pensioners (1.8 million) were living in poverty in 2014. Research by Age UK suggests that 900,000 of these pensioners are experiencing severe poverty, which is negatively impacting upon their health because they cannot afford decent food or to heat their homes. Fuel poverty is a particular problem. Age UK estimates that 2 million elderly people in 2014 were so anxious about their electricity and/or gas bills that they actually turned down their heating in the winter. The number of unnecessary deaths of elderly people due to fuel poverty was likely to exceed 40,000 per annum in 2015, according to the Department of Health.

Being old does not necessarily make people poor. Scase and Scase point out that a large minority of elderly people are affluent middle-class former professionals whose state pensions are topped up with generous occupational pensions and investments. However, they argue that the risk of poverty increases because of age. Many elderly people are forced to work past retirement age because they simply did not earn enough over their lifetime to put away savings or they worked for employers that did not run private pension schemes. Elderly women, in particular, are more likely to be in poverty than elderly men because they live longer and they generally receive less from earnings-linked private pension funds after taking time out of the labour market to raise children; consequently they did not contribute as much of their wage to this future benefit. There is also some evidence that the elderly may fail to claim the state benefits to which they are entitled because they are unaware of them or they are too embarrassed or proud to claim the money. Department for Work and Pensions statistics suggest that £2.8 billion in pension credit, used to top up pensioners' weekly income, was not taken up in 2011.

However, the number of elderly people in poverty has fallen over the last 30 years. Free bus passes, the winter fuel allowance and better state and occupational pensions have combined to lift many pensioners out of poverty. Nevertheless, the rapid ageing of the population suggests that poverty among the elderly will increase again because employers are now offering less generous pension schemes to the current workforce, while people have to work for a longer period before they receive the state pension. Those who work in low-paid zero-hour contract work are especially likely to experience poverty in old age.

Ageism

The elderly may be exposed to ageism, a process of negative stereotyping and discrimination. It takes several forms:

- Greengross argues that ageism has become institutionalised in that age barriers have been set by the state, which means that the elderly are excluded from many civic duties such as jury service. Similarly, in the NHS, older people may be subject to discrimination by being denied particular treatments or operations because of their age. Discrimination by financial services companies may mean that older people have difficulty obtaining insurance, getting a credit card or taking out a loan.
- Mass media representations of the elderly are also ageist. Carrigan and Szmigin argue that the mass media represent youth as beautiful and healthy while old age is frequently represented as the greatest threat to wellbeing. Both the mass media and the advertising industry create perceptions of old age as a time of dependency, poor health and poverty, despite the fact that this is not the experience of all the elderly. Ray et al. go further and claim that the elderly are often infantilised, ignored and treated in a patronising and disrespectful fashion by the mass media.

Exam tip

Ageism is something that is intersected by social class, gender and ethnicity. If you acknowledge this, it should earn you extra marks.

The young

Childhood can also be a dimension of inequality in that the young are very dependent upon adult society. This dependence means they lack an independent income and they are often powerless.

Poverty and social mobility

There is some evidence that the young make up a large subgroup of the poor. According to the ONS, 27% of children (3.5 million) were living in low-income families in 2013. Charities such as the Child Poverty Action Group and End Child Poverty have identified a number of consequences of poverty that particularly blight the lives of children and have a significant negative effect on children's chances of upward social mobility.

Children born into poorer households often have a lower birth weight than children born into better-off families and consequently are at greater risk of infant mortality and chronic illness later on in life. As they grow up, poorer children may not experience the same life-chances as their better-off peers. Poverty means that they miss out on holidays, school trips, technology and so on because their parents cannot afford these 'luxuries'. Moreover, the evidence suggests that poverty undermines schooling in that high-ability poor children do not attain the same level of qualifications as their better-off peers. For example, in 2011, children receiving free school meals achieved 1.7 grades lower at GCSE than their wealthier peers. Such children are more likely to leave school at 16 and more likely to be employed in precarious and casual low-skilled and low-paid work or to end up long-term unemployed.

In 2015, the youth unemployment rate (14.4%) was nearly two and a half times higher than the overall unemployment rate of 5.7% of the total population. The number of people aged 16–24 who were not in either full-time education or jobs numbered 498,000 — the highest figure for 20 years. However, some groups of young people face even greater unemployment rates because of their ethnicity.

There is also evidence that more young people are dependent upon their parents for a greater length of time. The increase in the value of property combined with low pay and/or employment — nearly a quarter of a million 18–20-year-old workers earn the minimum wage — means it is virtually impossible for some young people to get on the property ladder. Furthermore, the number of young homeless has increased.

Exam tip

Students often forget to discuss the young when they see questions on age. If the question is not focused specifically on the elderly, discuss the impact of ageism on younger age groups.

Summary

- Inequalities in wealth, income, poverty, educational opportunity and health undermine working-class children's potential for upward social mobility.
- There are distinct inequalities in the work experiences and opportunities of men and women, which negatively impact on women's health, education and social mobility.
- Evidence suggests that ethnic minorities experience significant barriers, which result in their under-representation in well-paid professional and skilled manual jobs and increase their potential to be unemployed and in poverty.
- The elderly often experience prejudice and discrimination, known as ageism.
- Children and young people are relatively powerless groups and consequently also experience specific types of prejudice and discrimination.

How can patterns and trends in social inequality and difference be explained?

The main sociological explanations of social inequality and difference

Functionalism

Functionalists such as Davis and Moore argue that stratification and inequality perform a positive function for society. This is because if societies are to operate effectively, they have to ensure that their most functionally important and senior positions are filled by people who are talented and efficient. The function of social institutions such as education is to allocate all individuals to an occupational role that suits their abilities (role allocation) via examinations and qualifications.

Role allocation produces stratification, however — in the form of economic and social inequality — because not all people are equally talented or skilled. Moreover, inequality is further increased by the fact that those in the top jobs are paid significantly higher salaries than those in other jobs. This inequality results in the emergence of different social classes.

However, from a functionalist perspective, stratification and class inequality are acceptable and, most importantly, beneficial to society. This is because functionalists believe that capitalist societies are essentially meritocracies in which people are rewarded for talent and hard work. It is thus important to have high rewards in the form of income and status and, therefore, inequality to motivate gifted people to make the necessary sacrifices. For example, they often have to spend long periods in education and training, often with little initial financial reward.

Even members of society who lack the qualities required for top jobs and who therefore occupy relatively low positions in the stratification system uncritically accept their social position. This is because they have been successfully socialised into agreeing that some jobs deserve higher rewards than others because they are functionally more important to the smooth running of society. As a result, people are generally happy to accept that surgeons deserve more economic rewards than hospital porters. This value consensus also means that most members of society believe that their own social class position is a fair reflection of their talent and ability. Consequently, functionalists believe that stratification is necessary and beneficial because it encourages all members of society to work to the best of their ability — those at the top will work hard to retain their advantages, while those below are motivated to work hard to improve themselves.

However, the functionalist theory of stratification has attracted several criticisms:

- Functionalists may have exaggerated the degree of consensus about rewards. There is evidence that there is substantial resentment in UK society with regard to the salaries earned by groups such as bankers and members of Parliament, especially as other occupational groups are subjected to austerity measures in the form of pay freezes.
- Unequal rewards may be the product of the power of some groups to increase their rewards regardless of so-called consensus. For example, the pay of company directors is set by them, not by society.

Exam tip

Never be content to include just one criticism. Aim to revise at least three critical points of each major theory.

Knowledge check 21

What is a meritocracy?

- The top of the stratification system is occupied not only by those with functionally important jobs, it is also occupied by those who live off inherited wealth and by celebrities. Neither of these two groups is necessarily functionally important to society.
- Evidence suggests that not all those who occupy top jobs are the most talented. They may have achieved their position because the UK is not really a meritocracy in which there is authentic social mobility. Family connections, the ability to pay for exclusive and expensive private education, the old-boy network, and hidden forms of institutional patriarchy and racism, rather than talent or ability, may have propelled the children of the white wealthy elite to the top.
- There are many occupations that are not highly rewarded that can be seen as functionally essential to the smooth running of society, such as nurses, water and sewage workers, refuse collectors and so on.
- Functionalists neglect the dysfunctions of stratification such as poverty, which negatively impacts on people and their mortality, health, education, standard of living and so on. Crime, riots and lack of community may be other dysfunctions of stratification systems.

Knowledge check 22

Identify five dysfunctions of stratification.

New Right

New Right thinkers such as Peter Saunders tend to believe that social inequality is the price to be paid for the fact that economic growth has raised the living standards of the majority of people in the UK and other Western nations. Saunders points out that even the poor are much better off today than they were in the past. He argues that capitalist societies have to offer incentives to those with talent and enterprise in the form of more income and wealth because these people are the innovators — the only ones capable of catching the public imagination with a constant stream of in-demand consumer goods such as smart phones and social media such as Facebook and Instagram. If these material incentives did not exist, talented people would not have been motivated to produce the consumer goods society takes for granted. In this sense, class stratification and the inequality that it produces is a necessary by-product of society's demand for the latest consumer innovations.

However, this New Right perspective has been criticised for generally neglecting the fact that social and economic inequality tends to result in envy, resentment and hostility among those at the bottom of the stratification system and might motivate them to engage in crime and social disorder.

Marxism

Marxists see all history as the history of class struggle. They argue that apart from a primitive form of communism that existed in early hunting and gathering societies, all stages of history have been characterised by stratification, specifically class-based societies.

Marxists see all capitalist societies as stratified by social class which is the product of the infrastructure or economic mode of production of a society. Modern capitalist societies have an industrial factory-based infrastructure in which companies compete to sell manufactured goods.

Marxists argue that the infrastructure is based on two components:

- The means of production refers to resources such as land, factories, machinery and raw materials, which are owned by a minority group — the capitalist class or bourgeoisie.

Exam tip

In any essay question on stratification or the causes of inequality, it is imperative that you mention the three theoretical giants in this field — functionalism, Marxism and Weber.

- The social relations of production refers to the relationship between the bourgeoisie and the working class or proletariat in which the latter hire out, in exchange for a wage, their labour power to the former.

Knowledge check 23

What is the infrastructure?

However, Marxists also argue that class inequalities in wealth, income and power are rooted in the infrastructure because it is in the interests of the capitalist class to keep wages low in order to increase profits. Moreover, the capitalist class exploits the labour power of the proletariat by controlling the organisation of work, for example by controlling the speed of assembly lines, and by appropriating the surplus value of the worker's labour power — that is, there is a significant gap between the wage paid to the worker and the value to the employer of the labour power of the worker which is pocketed by the bourgeoisie in the form of profit. Marxists, therefore, believe that class stratification and inequality are caused by the exploitation of workers by the bourgeoisie.

Neo-Marxism

Neo-Marxists focus on why workers are not often aware of class exploitation. They argue that workers experience false class consciousness — they have been fooled by another important component of capitalism, the superstructure, which is made up of ideological apparatuses such as education, the media, religion and so on, into believing that the class stratification found in capitalist societies is fair and natural. Neo-Marxists argue that the function of the superstructure is the reproduction and legitimation of class inequality through the transmission of ruling class ideology.

Althusser describes the educational system as an ideological state apparatus and argues that the idea that educational systems are meritocratic is a myth because the function of education is to legitimise the success of bourgeois children while working-class children are taught by schools to accept academic failure. Similarly, Bourdieu suggests that the children of the upper and middle classes are ensured educational and economic success because they have cultural capital — that is, the values and attitudes that teachers embrace — and economic advantages, for example, their parents can afford private education. Working-class children, meanwhile, lack cultural capital and are condemned to a life of manual work, most of them leaving education at 16. Nevertheless, they rarely blame the capitalist system for their 'failure' because the ideology of meritocracy ensures that they blame themselves. The organisation of capitalism therefore is rarely challenged and class stratification and inequality are reproduced generation after generation.

Other neo-Marxists such as the Frankfurt School have focused on the role of the media in creating a popular culture for the masses that has diverted working-class attention away from stratification and class inequalities towards consumerism, celebrity culture and trivia. Consequently, the proletariat pays little critical attention to political and economic life. Class inequality thus is rarely challenged.

Knowledge check 24

What is the function of the superstructure according to Marxists?

The Marxist theory of stratification, however, has been challenged:

- Marxism has been accused by its critics of economic reductionism. This means that Marxists see all inequality as the product of the economic relationship between the bourgeoisie and the proletariat. However, Weber in particular argued that inequalities and conflicts relating to nationalism, religion, gender and ethnicity cannot be adequately explained in exclusively economic terms.

- Marx did not really anticipate the rise of the middle classes and consequently their role in the stratification system.
- Marxist theory implicitly dismisses the working class as cultural dopes brainwashed by capitalist ideology.

However, evidence suggests that workers are aware of social class inequalities. Some have taken up the political fight against them while others believe that such inequalities are a lesser evil compared with the standard of living that capitalism has provided them with. The working class may be consciously reconciled to capitalism rather than falsely conscious or ignorant of how it produces inequality.

Exam tip

If you are faced with a question that focuses on 'functionalist' or 'Marxist' explanations of inequality, don't forget that you should always evaluate functionalism by contrasting it with Marxism. Similarly, Marxism should always be assessed by comparing it with functionalism and Weber.

Weberian explanations

Weber argued that the main cause of stratification is status differences. Status refers to the social standing of a group — how society ranks them in terms of prestige and importance. Weber agreed with Marx that status could be shaped by social class, but he also identified a number of other sources of status which he believed were just as important in bringing about stratification and inequality.

Weber defined social class in a qualitatively different way to Marx, in that he defined it in terms of market position, for example people's skills, qualifications, control over the work process, income and so on. This led to Weber pointing out that within broad social classes there exist groups that differ in status from each other. For example, some members of the working class are skilled workers — they are likely to have completed apprenticeships and qualifications and consequently they are paid reasonably well. These skilled workers therefore have more status than semiskilled, unskilled and unemployed members of the working class, which means they enjoy superior incomes and lifestyles.

However, Weber points out that in addition to social class, there are other sources of status inequality and stratification:

- There are examples of societies and communities in which people may acquire or be denied power, jobs and wealth because of their religious status.
- Some communities may discriminate against social groups and even persecute them because they belong to a different minority religion.
- In some societies, people may be regarded as having low status because of their skin colour and/or because they belong to an ethnic minority group that is the victim of racism.
- Status inequality may originate in belonging to a group that is able to exercise physical power over others, for example, many societies around the world are run by party or military dictatorships, such as those in North Korea or China.
- Many societies are patriarchal and judge females as having low status. Consequently women do not enjoy the same rights as males.

Knowledge check 25

What is economic reductionism?

Exam tip

Avoid the common error of confusing Marx and Weber.

Other sociologists influenced by Weber have attempted to explain the existence of racial inequality in the UK. Parkin, for example, notes that ethnic minority manual workers are technically part of the working class, but face racism in the form of prejudice and discrimination from the white working class. In this sense, they experience both status inequality and class inequality. Even middle-class Asian professionals may experience prejudicial attitudes from both the white middle and working classes.

Knowledge check 26

How does Weber categorise social class?

The Weberian dual labour market theory of Barron and Norris argues that the economy is divided into two sectors: the high-status primary sector made up of secure, well-paid jobs is dominated by white men, while the low-status secondary sector made up of low-paid, unskilled, part-time, insecure and zero-hour contract jobs is dominated by women and members of ethnic minorities.

Barron and Norris argue that women and ethnic minorities are less likely to gain the status of primary-sector employment because employers have sexist and racist beliefs about their unsuitability, and practise discrimination against them either when they apply for jobs or by denying them responsibility and promotion.

Employers often subscribe to stereotypical beliefs about the unsuitability of women workers. They may believe that women's careers are likely to be interrupted by pregnancy and childcare, and consequently may be less willing to train or promote them. Moreover, women may return to work part-time only because of the cost of childcare. Barron and Norris also point out that the legal and political framework protecting women from such prejudice and discrimination is weak. Relatively few employers have been prosecuted by the Equality and Human Rights Commission or found guilty of gender bias by employment tribunals. For example, in 2010–11, in employment tribunals only 37% of claims against employers for sexual discrimination were successful.

Similarly, Barron and Norris argue that the dual labour market is reinforced by the fact that the legal and political framework protecting ethnic minorities from discrimination is also weak. Of the 950 cases of employer racism investigated by employment tribunals between 2010 and 2011, only 16% were successful.

Meanwhile, Bradley criticises dual labour market theory because it fails to explain inequalities within the same sector. For example, teaching is not a secondary labour market, yet women are less likely than men to gain high-status jobs in this profession.

Some Weberians, especially Rex and Tomlinson, argue that ethnic minority experience of both class and status inequality has led to a poverty-stricken black underclass, which is marginalised and alienated and which has occasionally expressed its frustration in the form of inner-city riots.

The Weberian focus on status may explain the divisions that exist within social classes between both middle-class and working-class workers and between male and female white workers. It is particularly convincing in explaining the disproportionate number of ethnic minority workers who are either unemployed or employed in unskilled, low-paid work. However, the Weberian analysis has been criticised by Marxists for neglecting what they see as the most important exploitative relationship between capitalists and workers. Marxists argue that class and status are strongly linked because the capitalist class has status and power since it monopolises wealth and income, that is, because of its social class position. However, while Weber recognised that these factors overlap, he noted that a wealthy person such as a lottery winner can have lots of wealth but little status. Moreover, some people might have lots of status, for example a religious leader, but very little wealth or power.

Feminist explanations

There are a number of feminist theories which aim to explain gendered forms of stratification, including Liberal Feminism, Marxist-Feminism, Radical Feminism and triple-systems theory.

Liberal Feminism

Liberal Feminists argue that society is stratified by gender in the sense that men generally dominate the top jobs in societies such as the UK while women generally occupy subordinate positions. Liberal Feminists therefore focus on stratification as a patriarchal or male-dominated system.

Liberal Feminists argue that patriarchal stratification is mainly the result of (a) gender role socialisation and (b) ideology. First, Liberal Feminists such as Oakley argue that boys and girls are socialised into socially constructed gender roles. This means that societies such as the UK have clear ideas about what constitutes socially acceptable masculine and feminine types of behaviour. Children are taught this behaviour from a very young age by their parents as part of the primary socialisation process. Moreover, these gender roles are reinforced by the peer group, the education system, mass media representations and even religion. Gender role socialisation therefore reproduces a sexual stratification system in which masculinity is seen as dominant and femininity as subordinate.

Gender role socialisation is supported by a dominant patriarchal ideology, which also clearly prescribes and proscribes particular types of masculine and feminine behaviour that aims to reinforce patriarchal stratification. Oakley argues that the main reason for the subordination of women in the labour market is the dominance of the mother–housewife role. She notes the existence of powerful ideological ideas which serve primarily to ensure men's dominance of the labour market. For example, the ideology that children deprived of their mother's presence may grow up to be psychologically damaged functions to keep women in the home after having children rather than returning to work to compete with men.

In the 1990s, Liberal Feminists suggested that gender stratification was becoming less of a problem. Both Sue Lees' and Sue Sharpe's work on the attitudes of teenage girls suggests that education and careers are now a priority for young women, with females recently enjoying great educational success. Other Liberal Feminists have observed that women have made great progress in terms of the acquisition of economic power through careers, improvements in equal opportunities legislation, political power through greater representation in government, and social power through contraception and divorce. They believe, then, that patriarchal stratification is in decline.

However, not all feminists agree with this observation because both horizontal and vertical forms of job segregation by gender still exist. For example, in 2013, the Fawcett Society reported that men outnumber women four to one in Parliament, while only 15.6% of high court judges were women in 2013. Barron and Norris's dual labour market theory also undermines the Liberal Feminist assumption that better qualifications and changes in women's ambitions will automatically dismantle gender divisions in employment. In 2015, the gender pay gap was 14.6%.

> **Exam tip**
>
> Student responses that get top marks are the ones that avoid discussing 'feminism' in a generalised way and display knowledge of the differences between the various feminist theories.

Liberal Feminism has been criticised by Walby, who argues that although there is evidence that masculinity and femininity are socially constructed, this does not explain why men are usually in positions of dominance. Liberal Feminism also implies that women passively accept their gender identities. Finally, Liberal Feminism has been accused of treating women's experience of patriarchal stratification as a universal experience. Women's experiences may qualitatively differ according to their social class position as well as their ethnic and religious statuses.

Marxist-Feminism

Marxist-Feminists suggest that although gender stratification is important, it is not as influential as class stratification. Marxist-Feminists such as Benston argue that capitalism exploits both male and female workers, but as women are more likely to have children and work part-time, they are more likely to be part of a low-paid and often part-time 'reserve army of labour' hired by the capitalist class when the economy is prospering but laid off when recession sets in. This results in women being generally less skilled and relatively under-unionised compared with male workers. Marxists therefore argue that both horizontal and vertical segregation in jobs exist because women constitute a more disposable part of the workforce.

This weak occupational position is supported by a patriarchal ideology constructed by agencies such as the family and media that transmits the idea that women belong in the home rather than the workplace, which gives rise to influential ideas that men rather than women should be the family breadwinners. Moreover, when married women do lose their jobs, patriarchal ideology asserts that they have returned to their 'proper' jobs servicing their children and husbands.

Marxist-Feminism has been criticised for failing to convincingly explain why jobs are gendered, that is, why women occupy the housewife role or dominate certain sectors of work. If women are cheaper than men to employ, surely it would be more profitable for the capitalist class to replace the male workforce with a cheaper female workforce.

Radical Feminism

Radical Feminists suggest that gender stratification and inequality are far more important than other forms of stratification and inequality. Delphy, for example, argues that men and women constitute separate classes. These classes are organised around exploitation — men exploit women's labour power, especially in the family. This is done mainly via patriarchal ideology (for example, through ideas such as a woman's place is in the home, a real woman has children, children need their mothers and so on) and physical power — violence (for example, domestic violence, the threat of rape etc.). Radical Feminists see all social institutions as being characterised by patriarchy. However, the family is viewed as the main source of all patriarchal power because gender role socialisation plants the idea in children that males are dominant and females are subordinate.

Triple-systems theory

Sylvia Walby's 'triple-systems theory' is a variation on both Radical Feminism and Marxist-Feminism. Weber's ideas, too, have been incorporated into her theory. She suggests that patriarchal stratification has three elements to it:

Knowledge check 27

What is a reserve army of labour?

Knowledge check 28

Why is Liberal Feminism more optimistic in outlook than Radical Feminism?

Exam tip

You must be able to clearly differentiate between the different branches of feminism if you are to get into the top bands of the marking scheme.

1 Subordination: patriarchal institutions such as the family, media and education produce unequal social relations between men and women via gender role socialisation.

2 Oppression: women experience sexism because patriarchal ideology results in men discriminating against them.

3 Exploitation: men exploit women's skills and labour without rewarding them sufficiently, for example in the home.

Walby argues that patriarchy is not only about the interaction of men and women in these three respects but also intersects with capitalism and racism to produce gender stratification. Such inequality can be seen in six social structures:

1 The domestic division of labour within the family.

2 Vertical and horizontal segregation at work.

3 The patriarchal state, which acts in the interests of men rather than women with regard to taxation, welfare, weak equal opportunity laws and so on.

4 The failure of the law to seriously protect women from male violence such as rape and domestic violence.

5 Mass media representations of women in narrow and stereotypical social roles, such as sex objects, appendages of powerful males and mother–housewives.

6 Cultural double standards that endorse multiple sexual partners for men but condemn the same behaviour in women.

Catherine Hakim and rational choice theory

Catherine Hakim is critical of all the above feminist positions. She argues that feminist theories of gender stratification are both inaccurate and misleading. She argues that women are not victims of unfair employment practices because women with children make rational choices about their futures — they believe that childcare is just as important a career as employment. Consequently, the lack of women in top jobs and their domination of part-time work do not reflect employer discrimination, weak laws, gender role socialisation or patriarchal ideology but rather women's rational choice to be mothers and home-makers.

Knowledge check 29

Why is Hakim critical of feminist approaches?

Summary

- Functionalists believe that stratification is beneficial for society because it ensures that the most functionally important and senior positions in society are filled by the most skilled and talented, and motivates all sections of society to strive to better themselves.

- Marxists believe that stratification by social class only benefits the capitalist class, which has become powerful and wealthy by exploiting the labour of the working class.

- Weber claimed that other stratification systems organised around ethnicity, gender, religion and so on are just as important as those organised around social class.

- Feminists focus on gender stratification and patriarchal inequalities in employment, politics and so on, although different feminist schools of thought disagree on the cause of such disparities.

Questions & Answers

How to use this section

In this section you will find three questions at AS and three at A-level. Each has an A-grade answer with comments on the answers throughout. The question numbering for both the AS and A-level questions is the same as you will find in the examination. While the structure and mark allocation of AS and A-level are different, there is no harm in reading through and trying the 'other' questions — indeed, it will serve as good revision.

You should read each question carefully and either try to answer it in full or at least make notes of how you would answer it *before* reading the student answer and comments. This might help to pick up on mistakes you have made or things that you are doing well. Remember that there is no single perfect way of answering an exam question — the highest marks can be gained by taking different approaches, especially in the higher-mark questions. However, the comments should help to show you the kinds of approach that would do well and some of the pitfalls to avoid.

As a general point, you should always read through the whole question before starting to write. When you come to answer the question that is based on an item, read the item particularly carefully, as it will contain material that is essential to answering the question.

The student answers are accompanied by comments. These are preceded by the icon **ⓔ** and indicate where credit is due. Further guidance on each of the assessment objectives is given in the comments. The comments tell you what it is that enables the student to score so highly. Particular attention is given to the student's use of the examinable skills: knowledge and understanding; application; and analysis and evaluation. In practice, the grade-A answers, particularly those carrying the higher marks, will contain elements of all three assessment objectives (AOs).

Examinable skills

OCR sociology examination papers are designed to test certain defined skills. These skills are expressed as AOs and are the same for AS and A-level, though the weighting given to each differs between the two levels. There are three AOs and it is important that you know what these are and what you have to be able to do in an exam to show your ability in each.

Assessment objective 1

Demonstrate knowledge and understanding of:
- **sociological theories, concepts and evidence**
- **sociological research methods**

Your exam answers will have to demonstrate clearly to the examiners that your knowledge is accurate and appropriate to the topic being discussed and that you have a clear understanding of it. It is not enough simply to reproduce knowledge learned by rote — you must be able to use your knowledge of concepts, sociological studies, evidence and sociological theories in a meaningful and logical way to answer and illustrate with examples the specific question set.

Assessment objective 2

Apply sociological theories, concepts, evidence and research methods to a range of issues.

This means that you must be able to demonstrate the ability to address the question throughout your response by consistently applying relevant sociological concepts, studies and theories.

Some of the questions specifically focused on socialisation, culture and identity in the exam will instruct you to use the sources that precede the question — this may be a photograph, graph, piece of text and so on which sets the context for the question that is to follow and provides you with some information to help answer it. You *must* take this relevant information and use (apply) it in your answer. However, 'applying' the material does not mean simply copying it from the source and leaving it to speak for itself. You will need to show your understanding of the material by doing something with it, such as offering a criticism, explaining something about it, linking it to a particular sociological theory or using it as an example of what is being stated or suggested. You will also be expected to use your own knowledge to add to the information that you have been given and to apply it appropriately to answer the question.

Assessment objective 3

Analyse and evaluate sociological theories, concepts, evidence and research methods in order to:

- **present arguments**
- **make judgements**
- **draw conclusions**

The skill of *analysis* is shown by breaking something down into its component parts and subjecting them to detailed examination. Analysis is therefore shown by providing answers (depending, of course on what it is that you are analysing) to questions which instruct you to explain and to assess or evaluate specific sociological views or theories. It involves asking questions such as 'Who said or who believes this?', 'What does this concept relate to?', 'How was this evidence collected?' and so on. The skill of *evaluation* is shown by the ability to identify the strengths and weaknesses or limitations of any sociological material. It is not sufficient, however, simply to list the strengths or limitations of something — you need to be able to say *why* something is considered a strength or otherwise, and sometimes you will need to state *who* claims that this is a strength or weakness. Depending on what it is you are discussing, you may be able to reach a credible and supported conclusion about the relative merits or otherwise of something. This means that it should be based on the sociological arguments and evidence that you have presented during your answer.

Weighting of assessment objectives

In the exam papers, each AO is given a particular weighting, which indicates its relative importance to the overall mark gained. The weightings are not the same for

AS and A-level, so be sure that you look at the one that is appropriate for the exam you will be taking.

Component	Weighting for AS examinations		
	% of OCR AS in Sociology (H180)		
	A01	A02	A03
Socialisation, culture and identity (H180/01)	45–50%	30–35%	15–20%
Researching and understanding social inequalities (H180/02)	45–50%	25–30%	20–25%
Component	Weighting for A-level examinations		
	% of OCR A-level in Sociology (H580)		
	A01	A02	A03
Socialisation, culture and identity (H580/01)	40–45%	40–45%	15–20%
Researching and understanding social inequalities (H580/02)	30–35%	30–35%	35–40%
Debates in contemporary society (H580/03)	40–45%	20–25%	30–35%

Command words

Ofqual, the body that sets the criteria for all GCE sociology specifications, has an approved list of 'command words' that are used in exam questions. The following are some of the most commonly used, but it is important to remember that the list is not exhaustive and occasionally other, similar words or phrases may be used instead. All this shows how important it is to take time in an exam and read the questions very carefully before you start writing. It is worth learning what is meant by these command words, to ensure that you give an appropriate response.

Define Give the meaning of something

Explain Describe the purposes of something or give reasons for it

Describe/Outline Give the main characteristics of a concept or sociological view

Outline and explain Give the main characteristics of a sociological view and develop these by referencing studies and using examples

Using the source and your wider sociological knowledge, explain Draw on the material provided and develop it using your own knowledge to answer the question

Identify and briefly explain Recognise and give examples of something and explain its purpose or reasons for its existence

Evaluate/Assess Make judgements from the available evidence

■The AS examination

The topic of 'Researching and understanding social inequalities' is examined on Paper 2 of the AS examination, which is organised into two sections. Section A, which focuses on 'Research methods and researching social inequalities', contains two sources. Source A is likely to be a piece of data that demonstrates patterns and trends relating to some aspect of inequality and difference, while Source B is likely to contain detailed information about how a piece of research about inequality and difference was organised. Section A also includes four compulsory questions worth 4, 9, 12 and 20 marks respectively. You will be instructed to use Sources A and B to help you answer these questions, although most of your responses to questions 3 and 4 will depend on 'your wider sociological knowledge'. Section A questions add up to 45 marks altogether, or 60% of the paper.

Section B focuses on 'Understanding social inequalities' and will contain two compulsory questions worth 10 and 20 marks respectively. Section B questions therefore add up to 30 marks altogether, or 40% of the paper.

The whole exam lasts for 1 hour 30 minutes, carries 75 marks and is worth 50% of the AS qualification. It is worth spending about 50 minutes on Section A and 40 minutes on Section B. Try to manage your time so that you have enough spare to read through your responses to the whole paper at the end.

Question 1

Section A

Read the source material and answer all the questions in Section A.

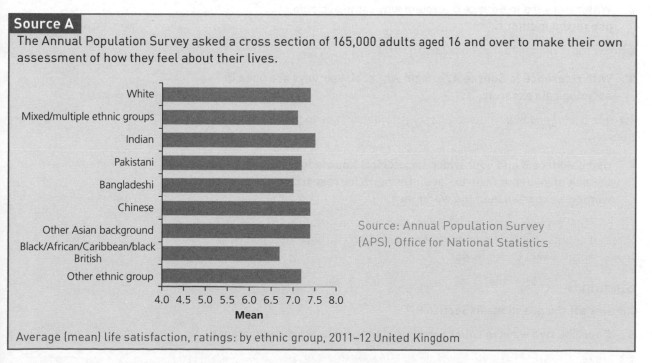

Source A

The Annual Population Survey asked a cross section of 165,000 adults aged 16 and over to make their own assessment of how they feel about their lives.

Source: Annual Population Survey (APS), Office for National Statistics

Average (mean) life satisfaction, ratings: by ethnic group, 2011–12 United Kingdom

Questions & Answers

The overall aim of this investigation was to understand more about the diverse experiences and aspirations of ethnic minority women in relation to work. The investigation focused particularly on Bangladeshi, Pakistani and black Caribbean women. Pakistani and Bangladeshi women were included because they have the lowest rates of employment of any other ethnic group, and black Caribbean women because they are under-represented in senior-level jobs.

The research design mixed a range of methods. Ethnic minority women were interviewed in groups in three British cities: London, Birmingham and Bristol. More in-depth face-to-face interviews were then carried out with ten Bangladeshi, black Caribbean and Pakistani women working in six organisations which employed ethnic minority women. Official statistics pertaining to these organisations and their policies were also collected.

The research revealed that 54% of black Caribbean women often had difficulty finding work (compared with only 34% of white women). It also found that increasingly black women are forced to take jobs below their skills and experience levels. Almost one-third (31%) of black Caribbean women had seen less experienced or less qualified people promoted above them and a third had experienced racist comments at work. The study concluded that despite a skills shortage, there is an under-utilisation of existing talent with regard to ethnic minority women. Caribbean women are clustered in the public sector, frequently in lower-level occupations than their experience or qualifications merit. Talent is therefore lost from an organisation if women leave because they feel they have been overlooked for promotion, especially when they see less qualified white men and women progressing more quickly.

Adapted from Bradley, H., Healy, G., Forson, C. and Kaul, P. (2007) *Workplace Cultures: What does and does not work*, Equal Opportunities Commission.

1   Describe **two** findings from the data in **Source A**.   [4 marks]

2   With reference to **Source B,** explain why some sociologists use mixed methods.   [9 marks]

ⓔ You must make clear reference to Source B.

3   With reference to **Source A,** explain why social surveys are used in sociological research.   [12 marks]

ⓔ Use a range of examples to display your understanding. Don't forget to refer to Source A.

4   Using **Source B** and your wider sociological knowledge, explain and evaluate the use of in-depth face-to-face interviews for researching ethnic minority women's experience of the workplace.   [20 marks]

ⓔ Start by explaining how such interviews work in practice. Identify and discuss their strengths and finally their weaknesses. Don't forget to integrate material from Source B into your answer.

Section B

Answer all the questions in Section B.

5   Describe **two** ways in which working-class people are disadvantaged.   [10 marks]

ⓔ Make sure you illustrate these disadvantages in detail.

6   **Evaluate the Marxist theory of stratification.**   [20 marks]

🅔 You will need to describe this theory in detail. It will need to include both traditional and neo versions of the theory. Evaluation means you should assess both its strengths and its weaknesses.

Student answer

Section A

1   The Annual Population Survey found that most life satisfaction was expressed by the Indian (an average score of 7.5) and white ethnic groups (7.4). In contrast, the least life satisfaction was expressed by the black ethnic group, which included black African, African-Caribbean and black British, who scored on average 6.7, although Bangladeshis were not too far behind with a mean score of 7.

🅔 Two findings are clearly identified. The student demonstrates an excellent ability to analyse and apply the raw data. **4/4 marks awarded.**

---

2   There are two main reasons why some sociologists use a mixture of research methods. Some will be interested in triangulation. They may wish to test the reliability of their research design and the validity of their findings from a questionnaire survey by asking people to keep a diary documenting their everyday experiences. They might also select a sub-sample and interview them.

A second reason why sociologists use mixed methods is demonstrated by Source B in which the researchers wanted to look at the experience of ethnic minority women at work from a number of different angles to give a full picture. Source B suggests that they used official statistics on employment as well as group interviews with a range of ethnic minority women. They then targeted six organisations and interviewed ethnic minority women in more depth about their experience of those organisations. This gave an in-depth picture of the experience of ethnic minority women in the workplace. This approach is known as methodological pluralism.

🅔 The student demonstrates excellent knowledge of the two main approaches to mixing methods. The first point on triangulation showed good rather than excellent knowledge because it needed to make more clear how the use of diaries and interviewing tested the reliability of the initial method or the validity of the findings. The student was more successful in the section on methodological pluralism and linked this convincingly to Source B. **7/9 marks awarded.**

---

3   Social surveys are the most common method used by positivist sociologists because they collect lots of quantitative data in a relatively short period of time from large groups of people. They normally use questionnaires or structured interviews to collect the data. Some social surveys are longitudinal, which means studying the same group of people over a long period of time. These are useful because they provide a clear image of changes in attitudes and behaviour, for example they are useful for studying educational progress and social mobility or, as in Source A, how satisfied ethnic groups are with life in the UK over a course of 2 years.

Social surveys are regarded by positivist sociologists as scientific. This usually means that they have the following characteristics. First, all respondents are subjected to the same stimuli because the questions are standardised. For example, in a structured interview, the interviewer merely reads out a list of questions and records the answer in a robotic way. They are normally not expected to deviate from the script or to ask extra questions. Therefore, all the ethnic minority women in Source A were probably exposed to the same questions.

Second, the questionnaire design should be objective — all leading or loaded questions should have been spotted and removed at the pilot survey stage. This dress rehearsal aims to remove all potential bias. Third, a random sampling technique should have provided a representative sample from which generalisations can be made. In Source A, it is highly likely that the 165,000 people who took part in the survey were randomly selected in some way.

Fourth, all these design elements should ensure reliability — another sociologist should be able to repeat the research with similar samples and obtain similar results. Finally, the closed questions used in most surveys should produce lots of quantitative data which can be converted into tables and graphs as per Source A, and compared and correlated. This then allows researchers to establish possible cause-and-effect relationships, for example the data on levels of satisfaction in Source A might be compared with other data on income, employment, housing and so on.

ⓔ The student has generally displayed excellent knowledge and understanding of why social surveys are used in sociological research. The response was accurate and detailed and included a range of knowledge in the form of concepts and theory. The information presented was relevant and substantiated. The student displayed an excellent ability to apply Source A to this question, and was focused throughout on social surveys. **12/12 marks awarded.**

4 In-depth face-to-face interviews are essentially unstructured interviews, that is, interviews in which a skilled interviewer informally asks open-ended questions about a topic such as experience of the workplace and allows the respondent to respond freely and in detail. Such interviews are essentially guided conversations in that the interviewer will have a list of topics to ask about but many of the questions asked will be responses to the answers given by the interviewees. A skilful interviewer in Source B will have flexibly followed up the responses of the women and probed their responses by asking them what they thought had caused their difficulties in finding work or obtaining promotion.

e A confident display of knowledge which clearly and intelligently explains how unstructured interviews work in practice and how they were probably used by the research cited in Source B.

> These types of interviews, which are normally carried out in the everyday naturalistic environment of those being researched in order to minimise the stress and artificiality of the method, are preferred by interpretivist sociologists who are concerned with understanding how people interpret the meanings or interpretations that underpin social life. The researchers in Source B intended to get inside the heads of the African-Caribbean women so that they achieved verstehen — an empathetic understanding of how these women experienced the workplace. An important aspect of the unstructured interview is gaining the trust of those being interviewed. The interviewer aims to establish a non-threatening rapport so that the interviewee feels comfortable communicating uncomfortable facts such as the experience of being the victim of racist practices. Source B suggests that this research was fairly successful in stressing that what the interviewee says or thinks is the central issue because detailed qualitative data was obtained relating to their feelings about being overlooked for promotion and seeing people with less experience being promoted over them.

e The student successfully links the use of unstructured interviews to theory and uses the concepts of naturalistic, verstehen and qualitative data accurately. There are also two reasonably good attempts to link the strengths of unstructured interviews to Source B.

> It is argued that unstructured interviews produce richer, more vivid and valid data than other research methods, especially if they are conducted by people with similar social characteristics to those being interviewed. For example, it is highly likely that many of the researchers in Source B were from ethnic minority groups.

e The speculation is a valid one.

> However, unstructured interviews are seen to have weaknesses. Positivist sociologists suggest that they are unreliable because they are not standardised, objective and quantifiable. Their reliability is also questioned because they also depend on a unique personal relationship between the interviewer and interviewee, and therefore cannot be replicated and verified by other sociologists. Such interviews are exceptionally time-consuming and consequently costly. Finally, all interviews are interactions and therefore there is always the danger that interview responses may be shaped by the interviewee feeling threatened by the status of the interviewer or being motivated by the desire to please the interviewer. All such responses may undermine the validity of the research results.

e The student successfully identifies and discusses a range of potential weaknesses of unstructured interviews, although it is a little list-like and it would have benefited from a reference to Source B. However, knowledge and understanding were generally excellent and the student scored the full 6 marks for this skill. A total of 4 marks were awarded out of a possible 6 for the references to Source B. Analysis and evaluation were a little under-developed but nevertheless good — 6 marks were awarded for this skill. **16/20 marks awarded.**

Section B

5 Working-class children perform much worse in education than all other social groups at all levels of the education system. For example, more working-class children leave school at the age of 16 with no qualifications than middle-class 16-year-olds. Connor and Dewson (2001) found that only one in five young people from working-class backgrounds participated in higher education.

Health across the population has improved over the last 30 years as can be seen in the increase in life expectancy, but the rate of improvement has been much slower for the working class. Generally, the working class experience poorer mortality rates and morbidity rates than the middle classes. Their life expectancy, especially in the north of England and Scotland, is significantly lower than their middle-class peers. Bottero notes that the lower your socioeconomic position, the greater the risk of low birthweight, infections, cancer, coronary heart disease, respiratory disease and strokes.

e The student demonstrates wide-ranging and excellent knowledge and understanding of two ways in which working-class people are disadvantaged. There is explicit and frequent use of sociological concepts and evidence for both ways. **10/10 marks awarded.**

---

6 Marxists are very critical of class stratification and class inequality. They argue that class positions (and therefore class inequality) are the product of the exploitation and ideology found in capitalist economic systems. Those at the top of society (the bourgeoisie or ruling class or upper class) exploit those at the bottom of society (the proletariat or working class).

e A succinct introduction.

Marx observed that UK society is a class society. The minority class — the bourgeoisie — owns the means of production (capital for investment, land, factories, technology and raw materials). The majority class — the proletariat — hires out its labour power to the bourgeoisie. This relationship between the bourgeoisie and the proletariat is known as the social relations of production. These relations are characterised by class inequality. The bourgeoisie exploit the labour power of the proletariat. They pay the lowest wages possible. Moreover, they pocket surplus value — the difference between the wage paid and the value the worker's labour has produced.

Surplus value is the source of the wealth held by the capitalist class and, therefore, the cause of class inequalities in wealth which then lead to class inequalities in income, power, education, health and so on. In particular, it is the cause of the poverty that exists in the UK.

e The student demonstrates an excellent understanding of Marxist theory. The response is logically structured and concepts are used accurately throughout this paragraph.

Neo-Marxists such as Althusser and Bourdieu argue that workers put up with this exploitation and inequality because of the superstructure. This refers to all the major social institutions, e.g. the family, education, mass media, politics, religion, culture etc. The function of the superstructure is to reproduce and justify the class inequality that exists in the infrastructure by transmitting ruling class ideology or ideas as 'common sense', 'natural' etc. For example, people are encouraged to believe that if they work hard, regardless of social background, they will get on, despite the fact that the evidence does not support this.

Neo-Marxists argue that the education system plays a major role in transmitting ruling class ideology. They suggest that education is a major ideological apparatus working on behalf of the capitalist class to justify inequality. This is done via the hidden curriculum — the working class learn to accept failure and a future of low-skilled and low-paid factory work. Marxists also see the mass media as a major ideological apparatus — it pushes celebrity culture and false needs to distract the working class from exploitation, alienation and inequality. Consequently the working class experience false class consciousness — they are unaware of their exploited status. Many are unaware of the degree of inequality in capitalist society, e.g. in the distribution of wealth. However, Marx believed that one day the working class would recognise their exploitation. They would become a class-for-itself and seek radical social change, i.e. revolution — but this has not happened.

e The student demonstrates an excellent understanding of neo-Marxist theory. The theory is applied accurately to the examples of education and the mass media. There is excellent use of concepts such as superstructure, ideology, alienation and false needs.

Marx's theory of class conflict was an extremely influential theory, for example it inspired revolutions in the USSR, China and Cuba — but it has been criticised for several reasons. First, the revolution in the UK predicted by Marx has not occurred. Second, Marx failed to predict the development and importance of the middle classes. Third, his critique of capitalism may be over-stated — capitalism has a fairly good record in regard to democracy, workers' rights, the welfare state etc. The working class may

> not be falsely conscious — instead they may be happy with what capitalism has provided them. Fourth, Weber criticised Marx for being an economic determinist — Marx sees social class as the most important source of inequality. Weber argued that gender/patriarchy, race/ethnicity, religion and so on are as important. Fifth, functionalists argue that stratification can benefit society because it encourages the most talented to compete for the top positions, increasing the society's efficiency.

ⓔ Evaluation should focus on both strengths and weaknesses. The former is rather superficial and the latter is list-like, although the student does accurately identify five very relevant criticisms. Overall this student displayed excellent knowledge and understanding of the Marxist theory of stratification and was awarded the full 6 marks for this skill. The student applied concepts and theory confidently throughout the response and was awarded the full 4 marks for application. Evaluation was explicit but was slightly under-developed and the student was awarded 8 marks out of a possible 10. **18/20 marks awarded.**

ⓔ Overall, this student scored 67 marks out of a possible 75 available on this paper.

Question 2

Section A

Read the source material and answer all the questions in Section A.

Source A

How people interpret their social class position: subjective social class, 1983–2012

	1983	1987	1992	1997	2005	2012
Subjective social class	%	%	%	%	%	%
Unprompted middle class	20	16	16	20	20	22
Prompted middle class	14	18	18	17	17	13
Unprompted working class	33	30	29	31	25	29
Prompted working class	27	31	30	30	32	32
Did not identify with a social class	6	5	6	2	6	5

Source: Park, A., Bryson, C., Clery, E., Curtice, J. and Phillips, M. (eds) (2013), British Social Attitudes: the 30th Report, London: NatCen Social Research, available online at: www.bsa-30.natcen.ac.uk

Source B

Simon Charlesworth: A phenomenology of working-class experience

Simon Charlesworth's ethnographic study focuses on working-class people in Rotherham in Yorkshire, the town where he grew up and lived while conducting the research. Charlesworth based his study specifically on 43 unstructured, conversational interviews, although he also clearly spoke to additional large numbers of people whom he knew socially. Many of the people to whom he spoke were male, but at least a third were female. There are also many observations scattered throughout the book as Charlesworth talks to people in natural settings such as the pub, the betting shop, on their council estates and so on.

Charlesworth claims to find social class seeping into all aspects of life in Rotherham. Generally, he found that miserable economic conditions such as recession cause working-class people to feel both physically and psychologically unhealthy. He found that the lives of working-class people in Rotherham were characterised by suffering and depression. For example, many unemployed workers experienced a lack of identity because of the loss of the status which normally accompanies paid work. Many of the teenagers saw no point in working at education or qualifications because even if they acquired them, they were not able to obtain decent work.

Charlesworth concludes that social and economic change have weakened people's sense of belonging to their working-class community. They have little hope for their future and they worry for their children. He claims that the socially excluded and deprived of Rotherham (which the locals called 'Deadman's Town') feel rage and suffering. The working-class culture that develops out of unemployment and poverty is one of having to make do and buy only what is necessary and cheap. It is therefore also marked by social and spiritual decay.

Adapted from Blundell, J. and Griffiths, J. (2002) *Sociology since 1995*, Vol. 2, Lewes: Connect Publications.

1   Describe **two** findings from the data in **Source A**.   [4 marks]

2   With reference to **Source B**, explain why sociologists use unstructured interviews.   [9 marks]

e   You must make clear reference to Source B.

3   With reference to **Source A**, explain why longitudinal studies are useful in sociological research.   [12 marks]

e   Use a range of examples to display your understanding. Don't forget to refer to Source A.

4   Using **Source B** and your wider sociological knowledge, explain and evaluate the use of ethnography for researching working-class experience and identity.   [20 marks]

e   Start by explaining how ethnography works in practice. Identify and discuss its strengths and finally its weaknesses. Don't forget to integrate material from Source B into your answer.

Section B

Answer **all** the questions in Section B.

5   Describe **two** ways in which ethnic minorities in the UK are disadvantaged.   [10 marks]

e   Make sure you illustrate in detail these disadvantages.

6   Evaluate the contribution of Max Weber to our understanding of racial inequality in the UK.   [20 marks]

e   You will need to describe Weber's theory in detail. It will need to include sociologists who have been influenced by Weber. Evaluation means you should assess both the strengths and weaknesses of Weber's ideas.

Student answer

Section A

1 Source A focuses on how people interpret their social class position in society. This is known as subjective awareness. The first trend that can be seen is that the majority of the sample identify themselves, whether prompted or not, with a working-class identity. This has hardly changed over a 30-year period. In 1983, 60% of people saw themselves as working class compared with 61% in 2012.

ⓔ The student identifies one finding only. **2/4 marks awarded.**

2 Unstructured interviews are interviews in which the interviewer informally asks open-ended questions about a topic and allows the respondent to respond freely and in depth.

   Sociologists like Charlesworth use unstructured interviews because they are excellent for studying sensitive subjects such as what it is like to experience poverty, unemployment, depression and so on. A skilled interviewer should be able to establish trust and rapport with interviewees and consequently obtain qualitative and highly valid data which should give insight into the daily lives of the research subjects. Charlesworth was able to gain the trust of the interviewees because he came from Rotherham and knew many of them personally. Charlesworth also informally talked to people in ordinary settings such as the pub and the betting shop, which probably also increased trust and the validity of the data. In contrast, methods like questionnaires and structured interviews are not normal features of everyday life and consequently people might not take them seriously.

   Interpretivist sociologists like unstructured interviews because they result in verstehen or empathetic understanding. This means the sociologist should be able to get inside the head of the research subjects and see the world through their eyes.

ⓔ The student identifies reasons why some sociologists prefer to use unstructured interviews. The material in Source B is used convincingly and concepts such as verstehen and validity are accurately applied to the analysis. The student is awarded 6 marks for knowledge and 3 marks for their use of Source B. **9/9 marks awarded.**

3 A longitudinal study is a survey which studies the same or similar groups of people over a period of years in order to monitor how much change is taking place in their lives. Source A is the product of the British Social Attitudes (BSA) survey which asks similar questions of a sample of the British population every 5–6 years.

If the group remains the same as in the television longitudinal survey of a group of children born in the early 1960s — *7 Up* — who have been returned to every 7 years, such surveys often produce in-depth and qualitative data about a group's life experiences because the research team can establish a trusting rapport with the group because of the frequent contact.

Longitudinal surveys are also regarded as useful because study over a period of time enables the study of large-scale social processes such as social class or poverty on educational, occupation and social mobility outcomes. Source A, for example, examines whether people identify with social class over a 30-year period. The data suggests that social class is still an important source of personal identity despite the great social change that has taken place in that period.

Longitudinal surveys are also useful because hypotheses can be modified during the course of such research in the search for the causes of social change on people's attitudes or behaviour. Finally, longitudinal studies are reliable in the sense that questionnaires and interviews can be repeated year after year and therefore produce directly comparable data. The BSA survey means we can compare data across three groups: the working class, the middle class and a group that does not identify with a social class identity.

e The student demonstrates excellent knowledge and understanding of six reasons why longitudinal studies are useful to sociologists and therefore scores the full 8 marks for this skill. The material in Source A is applied convincingly throughout the response and therefore the student is awarded the full 4 marks for application. **12/12 marks awarded.**

4 Ethnography is sociological research conducted in the natural environment of the research subjects, which aims to describe their way of life. It generally intends to give research subjects a voice, so data often composed of qualitative extracts from conversations or interviews, thus allowing the data to speak for themselves.

e This is an excellent and focused definition of ethnography.

Charlesworth's research was ethnographic — he spent a great deal of time in an economically deprived area (Rotherham) and aimed to give the poorest section of that community a platform from which they could describe and explain how they felt about living in poverty. Charlesworth was mainly concerned with validity — getting an authentic picture of how people experienced poverty.

His research methods were ethnographic in the sense that he lived among the community during the research period and was able to informally observe people in their everyday environment. He also conducted 43 unstructured interviews with residents, and had informal conversations with dozens of people he already knew from school and being brought up on a working-class council estate in Rotherham, in the pub and betting shop.

ⓔ The student accurately contextualises Charlesworth's research as ethnographic and links this convincingly to the concept of validity. There is also an excellent summary of the research approach in Source B.

> Charlesworth's research is essentially interpretivist, because he aimed to get inside the heads of his respondents and to experience the world of Rotherham from their point of view — he aimed to achieve verstehen, or empathetic understanding. He wished to see if people living in this area shared similar interpretations of their poverty and social class experience.

ⓔ The student makes an excellent link to the theoretical reasons for Charlesworth's approach to research. Note the use of the concept of verstehen.

> However, Charlesworth's informal conversations could be criticised for being unethical because people did not realise he was interviewing them. He did not seek informed consent. Charlesworth could also be accused of using and abusing friendship in order to obtain sociological data. Another problem was that he had to memorise conversations and write up his notes afterwards. Charlesworth's interview data can be questioned because it is his interpretation of what was said. He may have misrepresented some of his respondents because it is difficult to accurately recall whole conversations.

ⓔ Excellent points are made about the ethical side of the research, and evaluative issues of validity are raised.

> Another problem in Charlesworth's use of interviews was that it was unclear how people were sampled. Charlesworth's discussion of his research can be criticised for its vagueness in this respect. He tells us little about his respondents apart from their age and gender, and occasionally whether they are employed or not. It is unclear how many of his respondents were black or Asian. All these factors make it difficult to assess the validity of the data gathered.

ⓔ Sampling and access to the group are areas of the research that must be discussed. This is an excellent summary of the concerns about Charlesworth's access to the group being studied.

> We know that Charlesworth used unstructured interviews, which have some strengths. They allow the researcher to establish a relationship with the respondent, because they generally place the respondent at the centre of the interview. The unstructured interview is generally not rushed, but is paced according to the responses of the respondent. Interviewees feel that they have greater control over the direction of the interview and consequently talk about what they feel, rather than what the interviewer feels is important, making them

more likely to open up. These characteristics of the unstructured interview increase the respondent's trust in the interviewer, which generates more validity, in terms of richer, vivid and colourful data. Charlesworth states that this was his intention — he wanted the research to be a two-way process (a dialogue) in which the lives and language of the people of Rotherham could be recorded faithfully and authentically.

e This paragraph links a sociological discussion of the merits of unstructured interviews convincingly to Charlesworth's research.

However, Charlesworth may have had problems using unstructured interviews. They are time-consuming, and difficult to transcribe and analyse because of the sheer volume of material in the respondents' own words. Positivists might criticise Charlesworth's methods for being unreliable because such interviews depend on a unique relationship between the interviewer and interviewee that cannot be repeated and checked. There are also doubts about the objectivity of such interviews, as Charlesworth may have selectively quoted or interpreted material based on his own experience of living in the community.

e This discussion is focused on Charlesworth. Although it is easy to learn the strengths and weaknesses of particular methods, the real skill is linking it to the practical research, which this student does well.

The biggest problem with such interviews is interviewer effect or bias. Some people may have worked out from the questions he asked what answers he was hoping to hear and given him those responses. Some people may have attempted to manage Charlesworth's impression of them by avoiding giving answers that showed them in a poor light. For example, they may have been too embarrassed to answer questions on mental illness, depression or 'spiritual' feelings because they wanted to present themselves as socially respectable. Some respondents may have answered in particular ways because they wanted Charlesworth's approval. Consequently, they may have concealed or lied about aspects of their experience, therefore undermining validity. Finally, people are sometimes unaware that they are behaving in a particular way — interviews will not pick up this information.

e This section demonstrates excellent knowledge and understanding of interview bias.

Charlesworth also used the ethnographic approach of informal observation to compensate for the weaknesses of interviews. This is participant observation — Charlesworth attempted to immerse himself in the lifestyle of Rotherham people by living among them and hanging around the pub, the betting shop etc.

He hoped that this would give him an extra angle by giving him a first-hand view of poverty and therefore add to the overall validity of the study. However, there are drawbacks to using informal observation. Charlesworth might have 'gone native' and identified too closely with the residents, many of whom were his friends. Many of them probably knew he was an academic and they may have acted less naturally in his presence. The data produced by observation cannot be checked and therefore are seen by some as unreliable.

(e) The student recognises the importance of observation as an ethnographic tool and links it well to the aims of Charlesworth's research. There is also an excellent discussion of the potential problems Charlesworth might have faced using observation.

Overall, Charlesworth's study is a good example of interpretivist research using methods that often produce rich valid data, giving insight into how people feel about their situation. However, as with all studies that cannot be repeated, there may be some doubts about the reliability and objectivity of the study.

(e) This is an excellent response, which is focused on Charlesworth's research throughout. This student knows and understands both the theoretical and practical strengths and problems of using ethnographic research methods. The student also focused convincingly on problems relating to ethics, access and sampling. The student demonstrated excellent knowledge and understanding of ethnographic methods and is awarded the full 6 marks for this skill. The material in Source B was perceptively applied throughout the result. The student never lost sight of the study and consequently is awarded the full 6 marks for application. The student displayed an excellent ability to analyse and evaluate ethnography and particularly Charlesworth's use of it throughout the response and therefore the full 8 marks are awarded. **20/20 marks awarded.**

Section B

5 One way in which ethnic minorities are disadvantaged is in their access to jobs in the UK. Ethnic minority employees are concentrated in low-paying occupations such as sales, catering, textiles and so on and are more likely than white employees to be paid minimum wage. They are less likely to be found in professional or managerial jobs and when they are found in the latter group, they earn up to 25% less than their white peers.

Another way in which ethnic minorities are disadvantaged is in terms of poverty. A total of 40% of members of ethnic minority groups in the UK live in poverty. This is twice the poverty rate of the white British community. Over half of Bangladeshis, Pakistanis and black African children are growing up in poverty. Alcock argues that ethnic minority poverty has led to poor educational performance and the greater likelihood of living in overcrowded and poorly maintained rented accommodation in deprived areas.

(e) The student successfully identifies two ways in which ethnic minorities in the UK are disadvantaged. The level of detail is about right. The student uses percentages and trends to illustrate the degree of disadvantage. It is always a good idea to include a study. **10/10 marks awarded.**

6   Max Weber's theory of stratification differs from that of Karl Marx, who argues that social class is the most important source of inequality. Weber argued that the main cause of stratification and inequalities in wealth, income and power was status differences. Status refers to the social standing of a group — how society ranks them in terms of prestige and importance. Weber agreed with Marx that status could be shaped by social class, but he also identified a number of other sources of status such as race/ethnicity, gender, religion, physical and military power and so on, which he believed were just as important in bringing about stratification and inequality.

(e) The student begins by contrasting Weber's ideas with those of Marx, which demonstrates an excellent knowledge of the stratification debate.

Weber believed that ethnic inequalities in terms of access to jobs, unemployment, pay, education and health were caused by the fact that status and power are in the hands of the majority ethnic group. Weber therefore argues that racial inequality is a product of status inequality. He observes that white people generally have more economic, social, cultural and political power, and status than ethnic minorities. He acknowledged that ethnic minorities who do manual jobs are technically part of the working class, but Weberians such as Parkin point out that they are likely to face additional prejudice and discrimination from the white working class because they suffer from status inequality in addition to class inequality.

The Weberian dual labour market theory of Barron and Norris argues that the economy is divided into two sectors: the high-status primary sector made up of secure, well-paid jobs is dominated by white men, while the low-status secondary sector made up of low-paid, unskilled, part-time, insecure and zero-hour contract jobs is dominated by women and members of ethnic minorities.

Barron and Norris (1976) argue that ethnic minorities are more likely to be found in the secondary sector. They are less likely to gain primary-sector employment because employers may subscribe to racist beliefs about the unsuitability of black people — and even practise discrimination against them either when applying for jobs or by denying them responsibility and promotion. Furthermore, the legal and political framework supporting black people is weak. Trade unions are generally white-dominated and have been accused of favouring white workers and being less interested in protecting the rights of black workers. Various equality acts of Parliament which are supposed to protect black people from discriminatory practices are generally thought to be feeble.

> Another theory influenced by Weber was the underclass theory of Rex and Tomlinson, who argue that ethnic minority experience of both class and status inequality has led to a poverty-stricken black underclass. The life-chances of ethnic minorities are undermined by situational constraints over which they have no influence, such as institutional racism, employer discrimination, racism in general, globalisation and so on. Young members of ethnic minorities who are disproportionately affected by these factors feel particularly marginalised and alienated and occasionally express their frustration in the form of inner-city riots.

e The student successfully summarises Weber's ideas on status inequality and supplements them with accurate reference to sociologists such as Parkin, Barron and Norris, and Rex and Tomlinson who were very influenced by Weber.

> Weber's ideas have been very influential. It has been suggested that Weber has produced an adaptable 'history-proof' model of stratification that can explain all types of inequality. However, despite this, Marxists argue that racial/ethnic inequalities are usually symptoms of some deeper underlying class problem. Castles and Kosack argue that various forms of racism are deliberately encouraged among the white working class by the ruling class. For example, ethnic minorities and particularly migrants are often blamed and scapegoated for under-cutting wages, for white unemployment and for the decline of British cities. This 'divides and rules' the working class and sets white worker against ethnic minority worker, therefore diverting attention away from the main source of inequality — the exploitative nature of capitalism.
>
> Another Marxist, Miles argues that most ethnic minorities in the UK share the same class position as the white working class but they are treated as socially and culturally different by racist ideologies transmitted through the mass media which prevent their full inclusion and participation in society. Miles argues that ethnic minorities are members of 'racialised class fractions'. They are working class but prejudice and discrimination practised against them results in them stressing their ethnic and religious roots and culture in reaction. For example, some young Asians may react to deprivation and what they perceive as Islamophobia by turning to fundamentalist radicalisation.

e The student uses Marxism to explicitly and accurately criticise Weber's ideas.

> Finally, Weber has been criticised by Bottero, who argues that Weber fails to explain why societies supposedly organised around status conflict and inequalities are actually generally stable and orderly. Functionalists argue that stratification is not the negative phenomenon that Weber implies it is — rather, stratification is beneficial for society because it encourages all members of society to work hard to improve their social position.

e The student again demonstrates excellent knowledge and understanding of alternative theories of stratification and successfully uses these to evaluate Weber.

Overall this response demonstrated excellent knowledge and understanding of Weber and other theories of stratification. There was little more this student could have achieved in relation to this skill and therefore the full 6 marks for this skill was awarded. The student also scored the full 4 marks for application because the response never once lost its way. It was always focused on Weber even when discussing Marxism and other theories of stratification. The response had an evaluative tone from the very beginning and this was sustained throughout in a thoughtful and analytical way. A range of conceptual and theoretical points was raised and developed. The student was therefore awarded the full 10 marks for this skill. Overall the student scored the full marks for this response. **20/20 marks awarded.**

(e) Altogether, the student scored 73 marks out of a possible 75 on this paper.

Question 3

Section A

Read the source material and answer all the questions in Section A.

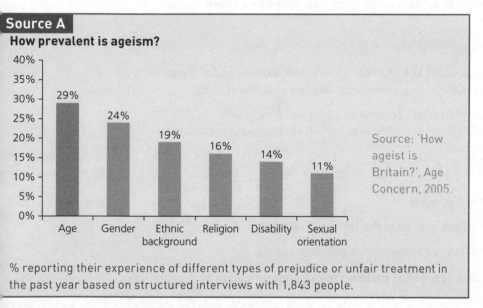

Source A

How prevalent is ageism?

Source: 'How ageist is Britain?', Age Concern, 2005.

% reporting their experience of different types of prejudice or unfair treatment in the past year based on structured interviews with 1,843 people.

Source B

Research commissioned by Age UK reveals that age is the most widely experienced form of discrimination in Europe. The European Social Survey (ESS) on ageism aimed to provide comprehensive quantitative data from a range of European societies using a representative random sample of people aged 15 or over and local sampling frames who were resident in private households in those countries. Pilot surveys were used extensively to test the reliability of the questions included in the final questionnaire. Nearly 55,000 individuals took part in the survey.

The research showed that ageism is rife in Europe — 64% in the UK and 44% in Europe believed that age discrimination against the elderly was a serious problem. In particular, the elderly faced the problem of subtle forms of prejudice such as the idea that older people are passive, needy and frail. Older people in the UK were more likely than their European counterparts to report that they had been treated disrespectfully or had been ignored and patronised. The report found that these subtle types of prejudice are just as harmful as overt discrimination because they make it difficult for older people to feel empowered and to be able to assert their preferences and choices.

Age discrimination was found to be a huge problem in the workplace. For example, the majority of those surveyed said they would find it easier to accept a suitably qualified 30-year-old as a boss than a 70-year-old with exactly the same qualifications.

Adapted from www.tinyurl.com/jga7sg5 (ESS4 2008)

Answer **all** the questions in Section A.

1   Describe **two** findings from the data in **Source A**.   [4 marks]

2   With reference to **Source B**, explain why sociologists use sampling frames.   [9 marks]

ⓔ You must make clear reference to Source B.

3   With reference to **Source A**, explain why structured interviews are useful in sociological research.   [12 marks]

ⓔ Use a range of examples and don't forget to refer to Source A.

4   Using **Source B** and your wider sociological knowledge, explain and evaluate the use of social surveys for researching attitudes towards the elderly.   [20 marks]

ⓔ Start by explaining how the social survey works in practice. Identify and discuss its strengths and finally its weaknesses. Don't forget to integrate material from Source B into your answer.

Section B

Answer **all** the questions in Section B.

5   Describe **two** ways in which women in the UK are disadvantaged.   [10 marks]

ⓔ This is asking for two detailed paragraphs. Use lots of examples.

6   Evaluate the contribution of feminist theories to our understanding of patriarchy in the UK.   [20 marks]

ⓔ You will need to describe feminist theories in detail. Evaluation means you should assess strengths and weaknesses of a range of feminist perspectives.

Student answer

Section A

1   Source A suggests that discrimination based on age, that is, ageism, is the most common type of prejudice or unfair treatment experienced by people in 2005 — 29% of the sample experienced ageism. In contrast, only 11% of the sample experienced prejudice because of their sexual orientation, making it the least likely type of discrimination to be experienced by the sample.

(e) The student successfully identifies and describes two findings from Source A. **4/4 marks awarded.**

---

2   Source B notes that the European Social Survey used local sampling frames in order to randomly select the 55,000 individuals who were resident in private households who took part in the research on ageism. These sampling frames were likely to be local electoral registers.

Sampling frames are important if researchers want to use a random sampling technique to select the sample they hope might take part in their research. Such frames are lists of names of people that sociologists can access such as the electoral register, which contains the names of people eligible to vote in elections. Once a sociologist has obtained a sampling frame, he or she will adopt a random sampling technique to extract a sample from the frame. The aim is to achieve a sample that is representative of the bigger group to which the sample belongs. Representative means that the sample should be a good cross-section of the group the sociologist is studying and that it should reflect its characteristics in terms of gender, age, social class, ethnicity and so on.

It is therefore important to find a complete sampling frame, otherwise whatever random sampling method is adopted is likely to lead to a biased sample.

(e) Although this response is generally accurate, it scored only 4 marks out of a possible 6 for knowledge and understanding because it demonstrated only good rather than excellent knowledge. It was a little under-developed in that it needed to discuss the range of sampling frames that is available to the sociological researcher. It was not made entirely clear why samples need to be made representative. More, too, could have been made of Source B, for example by describing the type of person who was sampled by the ESS in terms of age. Consequently only 2 marks were awarded for this skill. **6/9 marks awarded.**

---

3   Source A is composed of a table which summarises the findings on prejudice and unfair treatment experienced by a sample of 1,843 people on the basis of criteria such as age, race, disability and gender. This data was obtained by Age Concern by carrying out structured interviews.

Structured face-to-face interviews are mainly composed of closed questions and the interviewer behaves as much like a machine as possible. He or she is not usually allowed to deviate from the questionnaire or probe the research subject by asking extra questions. Instead, their job is to read out the questions and record the answers by ticking the appropriate boxes. This is a positivist research method and the emphasis is on gathering quantitative data in the form of statistics.

Positivists regard structured interviews very highly because they involve the use of standardised questionnaires and are consequently objective

---

and reliable. If the interview schedule is well designed, other researchers interested in ageism ought to be able to repeat the interviews in order to verify the results.

Such interviews are also advantageous because they can be carried out relatively quickly and cheaply. The former means that they are also customer friendly in that people may not mind too much spending 5 minutes being interviewed. Finally, some researchers encourage their interviewers to add to the survey data by observing responses to the questions in terms of facial expression, tone of voice, body language and so on.

🅔 Good knowledge and understanding was demonstrated regarding structured interviews but they were under-developed. The student produced a good description of how the structured interview works in practice, but the discussion of its strengths as a method required more depth and illustration. For example, the student identified a limited number of reasons why positivists prefer the method and it wasn't clear why some researchers encourage interviewers to observe the interviewees. Furthermore, apart from the introduction, Source B was not used to illustrate why some sociologists prefer the structured interview. The student scored 5 marks for knowledge and understanding and 2 marks for application. **7/12 marks awarded.**

4 Social surveys involve the systematic collection of the same type of data from a fairly large number of people. Social surveys usually obtain this information through questionnaires or, less often, through structured interviews. The information is then analysed using statistical techniques. Social surveys usually aim to find out facts about the population. For example, the European Social Survey (ESS) on ageism described in Source B aimed to provide comprehensive quantitative data from a range of European societies. A total of 55,000 people were surveyed using local sampling frames such as local electoral registers. The survey questionnaire was designed in order to ask a range of questions relating to various types of age-related overt prejudice and discrimination, including workplace experience as well as more subtle and hidden prejudice such as that contained in patronising language. The survey confidently reported that ageism was rife across the whole of Europe and that the elderly in the UK were more likely than their European counterparts to report that they had experienced ageist treatment.

🅔 This is a promising beginning. The student rightly begins by describing how social surveys work in practice and describes in excellent detail how the research in Source B is organised.

Questionnaires are the main method used in surveys. They are usually handed to people for self-completion or sent through the post. They are often made up of closed questions with fixed-choice tick-boxes attached which produce quantitative data. Questionnaires have a number of practical strengths. First, they can be distributed to very large samples because this increases representativeness and the possibility of generalising to the wider population. The ESS survey, for example, used a sample of 55,000 people scattered across Europe. Second, questionnaires are less time-consuming and costly than other methods.

Positivists are very keen on using survey questionnaires because they see them as scientific because they are thought to be objective and highly reliable. Another researcher using the same questionnaire on similar samples of people should achieve similar results. Positivists also like the fact that questionnaires produce lots of quantitative data which can be compared, correlated and presented in table, chart or graph form. Finally, positivists argue that questionnaires produce highly valid data because everyone is answering the same questions, therefore any difference in responses should truly reflect differences in real life.

(e) This is an excellent section focused on both the practical and theoretical reasons for using questionnaire surveys.

However, interpretivist sociologists have raised a number of practical, ethical and theoretical objections to questionnaires. First, it is practically difficult to go into any depth in a questionnaire about people's motives, feelings etc. This is because they often use closed questions with fixed-choice tick-boxes which allow few chances for elaboration. Second, questionnaires often suffer from non-response or low response, which can undermine the representativeness of the research.

Interpretivists believe that the data collected by questionnaires lacks validity for two reasons. First, people may interpret the same questions in different ways to that intended by the researcher. Second, the sample may deceive the researcher because they feel threatened by the research or they may feel that the researcher might disapprove of their behaviour. Validity is therefore undermined because people like to manage the impression other people have of them. For example, some people in the ESS survey may not have wanted to reveal their sexuality or admit to being a 'victim'.

(e) The student demonstrates excellent knowledge of the pitfalls of using questionnaire surveys, although the use of the ESS survey as illustration is a little basic. It is recommended that rather than use general terms such as 'people', students should think about how the research population used in Source B might have specifically experienced the identified problems. For example, what problem of interpretation might have been caused by the fact that the questionnaires were translated into several European languages? Why might a survey on a problem like ageism produce invalid responses? The student was awarded 5 marks for knowledge and understanding, 3 marks for application and 5 marks for evaluation. **13/20 marks awarded.**

5 Women in the UK are disadvantaged in terms of their employment experience. It is argued that they experience vertical segregation in jobs. This means that within occupational groups, women tend to be concentrated at the lower levels. Moreover, they often experience a 'glass ceiling' — a situation in which promotion appears to be possible but is prevented by stereotypical attitudes held by employers and discriminatory actions.

Women in the UK are also disadvantaged by the existence of a pay gap between men and women, which in 2014 stood at 19% measured by gross hourly pay. Some feminists argue that this pay gap is the result of a 'maternity penalty' — women spend long periods of time in the home raising children. The return to paid work may mean that women are disproportionately found in low-paid, part-time and temporary, casual forms of work.

e The student successfully identifies two ways in which women are disadvantaged, although the knowledge is good rather than excellent because it is slightly under-developed. For example, it would have improved the response if examples of employer stereotypical attitudes or discriminatory actions had been cited or the 'maternity penalty' had been explained in full. **7/10 marks awarded.**

6 Feminist theories of society see modern capitalist societies as patriarchal. They argue that the social institutions that make up society such as the family, education, mass media, religion and the economy function to bring about a social system in which men dominate economic and social power while women mainly dominate subordinate positions. There are three feminist theories which aim to explain patriarchy: Liberal Feminism, Marxist-Feminist and Radical Feminist.

e A promising introduction, which identifies the primary motivation of feminist theories — the desire to explain patriarchy — and identifies the three major types of feminism.

Liberal Feminists argue that patriarchy is caused by two factors. First, Ann Oakley argued that gender role socialisation into masculine and feminine values and roles means that parents indoctrinate male and female children into believing males are superior to females. She claims that for generations, female children have been less valued than male children and directed towards home and family and away from education and careers. Second, men's domination of the worlds of work, politics, law, religion and so on means that males were able to build barriers which prevent women from achieving equality. However, Liberal Feminists argue that women's position in UK society is improving because the needs of the economy have changed, resulting in the feminisation of the workforce, and the state has outlawed employer discrimination towards females in job recruitment.

Wilkinson argues that women's social attitudes and aspirations have undergone radical change compared with previous generations, while Sharpe argued that the present generation of young women see themselves as equals to men.

Liberal Feminists therefore see equality between men and women as a very real possibility. However, they are still concerned that some patriarchal inequalities continue to persist, e.g. domestic violence, women's lack of representation in Parliament and the differences in pay.

e The student demonstrates excellent knowledge and understanding of Liberal Feminism but there is implicit evaluation included in the reference to the persistence of patriarchal inequality.

Another type of feminism is Marxist-Feminism. They see the organisation of capitalist societies as primarily resulting in both social class inequalities and patriarchal inequalities. Marxist-Feminists see capitalist society as deliberately constructing conflict between men and women in order to distract from the more important social class inequalities caused by capitalist exploitation.

e The section on Marxist-Feminism is disappointing because although it links capitalism to patriarchy, it fails to explain how this relationship works in practice. The response needed to focus on how women are treated in capitalist societies according to Marxist-Feminists such as Benston. There is also no evaluation of the theory.

Radical Feminists claim that all societies, whether they are capitalist or not, are patriarchal. They argue that patriarchy existed well before capitalism appeared in the eighteenth century. They argue that men and women constitute sex-classes that are in fundamental conflict with one another. Furthermore, they argue that patriarchy benefits all men.

Kate Millett and Shula Firestone argue that men and women have very different interests, and that men exploit women in the family, government, religion, law, education and the media. Radical Feminists also believe patriarchal ideology is used to control women for the benefit of men. Women are told how to look, dress and behave. They are encouraged to believe that it is normal and natural for women to have less influence and power than men. Radical Feminists argue that when ideology fails, males use violence to control women.

However, Radical Feminism has been criticised too for failing to consider recent economic, political and social changes which have led to women now having a wide range of choices in the twenty-first century.

e The section on Radical Feminism is an improvement compared with the section on Marxist-Feminism. However, the knowledge demonstrated is good rather than excellent because it is slightly under-developed. For example, it was not clear where men's power originates or what forms men's exploitation of women takes or how ideology works in practice. Evaluation, too, was thin and important criticisms of Radical Feminism such as that of Hakim were omitted. The student was therefore awarded 4 marks for reasonably good knowledge and understanding, 3 marks for application and 4 marks for evaluation. **11/20 marks awarded.**

e The student scores a total of 48 marks out of the 75 available for this paper.

■ The A-level examination

The topic of 'Researching and understanding social inequalities' is examined on Paper 2 of the A-level examination, which is organised into two sections. Section A, which focuses on 'Research methods and researching social inequalities', contains two sources. Source A is likely to be a piece of data that demonstrates patterns and trends relating to some aspect of inequality and difference, while Source B is likely to contain detailed information about how a piece of research about inequality and difference was organised. Section A also includes four compulsory questions worth 4, 6, 10 and 25 marks respectively. You will be instructed to use Sources A and B to help you answer these questions, although most of your responses to questions 3 and 4 will depend on 'your wider sociological knowledge'. Section A questions add up to 45 marks altogether, or 43% of the paper.

Section B focuses on 'Understanding social inequalities' and will contain two compulsory questions, worth 20 and 40 marks respectively. Section B questions therefore add up to 60 marks altogether, or 57% of the paper.

The whole exam lasts for 2 hours 15 minutes, carries 105 marks and is worth 35% of the A-level qualification. It is worth spending about 60 minutes on Section A and 75 minutes on Section B. Try to manage your time so that you have enough spare to read through your responses to the whole paper at the end.

Question 1

Section A

Read the source material and answer all the questions in Section A.

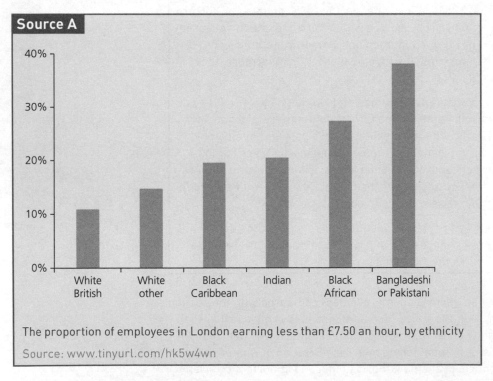

The proportion of employees in London earning less than £7.50 an hour, by ethnicity

Source: www.tinyurl.com/hk5w4wn

Source B

For many families in the UK, paid work does not lift them out of poverty because of low pay. Several ethnic groups are known to have a high proportion of minimum wage workers — particularly Bangladeshis, Pakistanis and migrant workers. This research aimed to clarify the links between the poverty experienced by working adults, the role of ethnicity and the contribution of informal workplace cultures to opportunities for progression beyond low-paid work and out of poverty.

This was a qualitative study. Fieldwork was undertaken in four urban and semi-rural areas in England and Scotland, from July 2012 to February 2013. Nine workplaces were chosen. In-depth unstructured interviews were undertaken with 43 managers and 65 low-paid workers from a range of ethnic backgrounds, including ethnic minority groups and white British.

The research found that a number of barriers were encountered by low-paid workers from ethnic minority groups. Management were often complicit in constructing these barriers. Informal behaviour and practices, such as prejudice and typecasting, contributed to ethnic minority workers feeling excluded from opportunities such as training courses that might lead to promotion. UK-born employees from ethnic minority groups faced under-recognition of their skills and experience, while recent migrants encountered non-recognition of their overseas qualifications.

Across all ethnicities, worker accounts suggested that opportunities for promotion and training for some low-paid workers were strongly shaped by personal relationships with supervisors and line managers. Good relationships with managers meant being favourably considered for developmental opportunities and promotion. Some ethnic minority workers felt that ethnicity was a clear dynamic at play. One worker observed: 'This one person came to the service, who had only been in the service for 2 years, and there was this job going as a manager. There had been so many people applying for it who had been in the service for a very long time … I mean the guy might have been good at his job, but there were [non-white] people who were better. But he was very close to one of the managers. Funnily he got the job and the rest were you know…'

These worker accounts suggest that these pockets of informal practice in the workplace are negative and undermining to equal opportunities. They affected ethnic minority workers disproportionately and strengthened low-wage traps. This contributed to underemployment and wasted potential. Such unequal treatment was often hidden and under-reported because of workplace contexts that bred a reluctance to complain to management or trade unions.

Adapted from the source: In-work, poverty, ethnicity and workplace cultures, M. Hudson *et al.*, Joseph Rowntree Foundation, September 2013.

1 Summarise the data shown in **Source A.** [4 marks]

ⓔ Don't forget to illustrate with examples.

2 With reference to **Source B,** explain **two** reasons why some sociologists use qualitative studies when conducting sociological research. [6 marks]

ⓔ Don't forget to illustrate with reference to Source B.

3 With reference to **Source A,** explain **one** strength and **one** weakness of using secondary data to study low income. [10 marks]

ⓔ Make sure each strength and weakness is detailed and is illustrated by a reference to Source A.

4 Using **Source B** and your wider sociological knowledge, assess the usefulness of unstructured interviews for investigating the relationship between ethnicity and workplace practices. [25 marks]

ⓔ Describe the method and explain how it works in practice before describing and assessing its strengths and weaknesses.

Section B

Answer all the questions in Section B.

5 Outline ways in which poverty may impact upon ethnic minority life-chances in the UK. [20 marks]

ⓔ It is important to be detailed and to include reference to a reasonably wide range of ways.

6 'Ethnicity and gender are just as important as social class as a source of inequality.' Discuss. [40 marks]

ⓔ Note the question includes reference to three concepts: ethnicity, gender and social class. It is important to get the balance right between them. The response should mainly focus on theories of stratification.

Student answer

Section A

1 Source A refers to the percentage of workers earning £7.50 an hour or less in London between 2007 and 2009. The table indicates that white workers were more likely to earn over £7.50 than all ethnic minority groups. In contrast, the group most likely to earn £7.50 or less an hour was the Pakistani/Bangladeshi group — nearly 40% of this group was low-paid. African-Caribbeans and Indians were the minority groups less likely to be found in this pay bracket — only 20% of these groups were paid less than £7.50 an hour.

ⓔ The student shows excellent ability by clearly summarising the data in Source A. **4/4 marks awarded.**

2 Qualitative data is data which speaks for itself because it is made up of interview transcriptions as well as quotes from conversations and diary entries. It is preferred by interpretivist sociologists because it gives a first-hand and therefore highly valid account of how people interpret their social reality. Another reason why qualitative data is used is that it supports quantitative data, which tells sociologists about trends and patterns. Qualitative data can explain the motives and reasons why the statistical data is the way it is.

e Although the student identifies two relevant and detailed reasons why some sociologists like to use qualitative data, they make the common error of failing to relate either of these to Source B. **2/6 marks awarded.**

---

3 A strength of using secondary data to study low income is that official statistics have normally been collected in a scientific way. In other words, the state has used standardised, objective and reliable criteria to collect statistical data on low pay. However, interpretivists are critical of statistical forms of secondary data because the state may not be using the same definitions and criteria as those normally used by sociologists. For example, the state definition of poverty used in Source A may differ from that used by sociological surveys of poverty.

---

e This is an accurate description of a strength and a weakness of secondary data but it is slightly under-developed. For example, the student could have explained what is meant by 'standardised, objective and reliable' or explained how a sociological definition of poverty might have differed from an official definition. Also, there is only one brief reference to Source A. The student is awarded 2 marks for application and 4 marks for evaluation. **6/10 marks awarded.**

---

4 Unstructured interviews are interviews in which the interviewer informally asks open-ended questions about a topic and allows the respondent to respond freely and in depth. The interviewer does not have an interview schedule or questionnaire. In Source B, Hudson will have some general questions about ethnic minority experience of the workplace and poverty, but he or she will have been flexible and willing to follow the lead of the person who is being interviewed. A good unstructured interview will feel like a conversation and the interviewer will have very good interpersonal skills and will be able to encourage people to talk at length.

---

e A good introduction which explains how the method works in practice. There is an excellent application of Source B.

Unstructured interviews are excellent for studying sensitive subjects, such as in Source B, a person's experience of racism in the workplace, because a skilled interviewer should be able to establish trust and rapport over the course of the interview and obtain qualitative data high in validity, which should give insight into how people interpret their experiences of racism or poverty. The evidence from Source B suggests that the interviewers were successful in that ethnic minority workers were able to give lots of examples of informal and hidden prejudice and typecasting that characterises their relationship with managers as well as giving interviewers examples of prejudice they did not report.

---

e This is very focused on Source B.

Interpretivists are keen on unstructured interviews because they believe in validity through involvement — valid data can be obtained only by getting close to people's experiences and meanings. Interpretivist sociologists like unstructured interviews because they result in verstehen or empathetic understanding. This means the sociologist should be able to get inside the head of the research subjects and see the world through their eyes. The data collected is normally qualitative and therefore rich in detail. The research subjects are given the opportunity to express how they feel in their own words. In Source B, qualitative data in the form of quotations is used to illustrate how ethnic minority workers believed that 'ethnicity was a clear dynamic at play' in their opportunities for training and promotion.

Unstructured interviews place the research subjects at the centre of the research process and make them feel that their point of view is important. This can lead to new insights being uncovered as people open up and say what they really feel and mean, which further increases validity. The interviewer can also probe vague responses and check with the interviewees that they share and have truly understood the meaning of what they have said. New hypotheses may result from understanding life in the workplace from an ethnic minority worker's point of view.

(e) The student demonstrates excellent knowledge of interpretivism and continues to use Source B as illustration.

Positivist sociologists don't like unstructured interviews because they see them as unreliable. They cannot be repeated and their data checked and verified because they are the product of a unique relationship between the interviewer and interviewee. They also claim that such interviews are rarely objective because interviewers often become over-friendly with their research subjects.

(e) The student rightly sees the need to contrast interpretivism and positivism.

A major potential problem of all types of interview is 'demand characteristics', which refers to those participants who attempt to work out what the researcher wants and consequently unconsciously change their behaviour or responses. The data collected from such research situations will no longer reflect natural behaviour and may therefore be low in validity. For example, some respondents in their eagerness to please the interviewer may give the interviewer the replies they think the sociologist wants rather than the truth. This is known as the social desirability effect. It is possible that the workers interviewed in Source B gave researchers examples of what they thought the researchers wanted to hear or exaggerated accounts of workplace racism.

Another major problem with interviews is that interviewees may be affected by the status of the interviewer. It is important to minimise the social and power differences between the interviewer and interviewee in order to increase the level of trust. For example, it is likely that the researchers interviewing ethnic minority workers were from similar backgrounds whereas white interviewers were probably used to interview white managers.

However, if pilot interviews were conducted and interviewers were well trained, it is likely that a research team such as that of Hudson in Source B will have taken on board all these potential problems and reduced the possibility of interview bias and therefore increased the validity of the data they collected.

e The student demonstrates excellent understanding of the interpretivist critique throughout. The application of Source B is first class.

Finally, it is important to consider that interviewing depends on what people know about their own behaviour. Obviously, this may be affected by faulty or hazy memory, but sometimes people simply do not recognise that they behave in a particular way. Consequently, there may be a gap between what people say they do and what they actually do in practice. For example, although managers were interviewed according to Source B, it is highly likely that they would have denied behaving in racist ways. However, they may not have recognised that their behaviour was racist.

Some sociologists may adopt mixed methods to counter this problem. They may use triangulation or multiple methods to either cross-check the validity of their data or to look at the problem from multiple angles to get a fuller picture of the problem. For example, long-term observation may show that managers do treat some ethnic minority groups more negatively. The Hudson study in Source B attempted to address this by using four different locations.

e The student identifies potential problems and quite rightly attempts to propose solutions. This student demonstrates excellent knowledge and understanding throughout the whole response and is therefore awarded the full 5 marks for this skill. The student showed an excellent ability to apply sociological theories, concepts and evidence to the uses of unstructured interviews in sociological research. The student explicitly applies material both from Source B and from elsewhere, and therefore scores the full 5 marks for this skill. Finally, the student shows an excellent ability to evaluate and analyse the usefulness of unstructured interviews for researching the relationship between ethnic inequalities and workplace practices. The student scores the full 15 marks for this skill. **25/25 marks awarded.**

Section B

5 Poverty negatively impacts upon ethnic minorities in the UK in a variety of ways. Research by the Joseph Rowntree Foundation in 2007 showed that 40% of ethnic minority communities in the UK live in poverty — double the poverty rates of white communities. Half of all ethnic minority children in the UK live in poverty. In 2015, Fisher and Nandi's research concluded that

Pakistani and Bangladeshi groups, followed by black African and black Caribbean groups, were the groups most likely to be found in persistent poverty. They found that 37% of Pakistanis were in poverty for two consecutive years and 14% in poverty for three consecutive years. Only a third (32%) of Pakistanis and Bangladeshis did not experience poverty in the period 2009 to 2012.

Poverty is often caused by unemployment and/or low wages. In 2004, official statistics showed that ethnic minorities generally earn lower incomes than white people, on average £7,000 less per year. Those of African-Caribbean origin and a majority of those of Asian origin have a greater chance of earning lower wages than the majority population, and they are more likely to work in the types of employment where wages are generally low. The Joseph Rowntree Foundation found that ethnic minorities in managerial and professional jobs earnt up to 25% less than their white colleagues. The Labour Force Survey of 2011–13 found that in London 44% of Bangladeshis and Pakistani employees were paid below the living wage compared with only 20% of white employees.

Alcock points out that poverty has a number of negative effects on the life-chances of ethnic minorities in the UK. First, 70% of all ethnic minorities in the UK live in the 88 most deprived districts compared with only 40% of the general population. They are also more likely to live in poor quality and overcrowded housing. Second, there is some evidence that ethnic minorities living in the inner city are over-zealously policed and that this has led to poor community–police relations, which has sometimes resulted in urban disorder. Third, ethnic minorities are more likely to attend failing schools in inner-city areas. Poverty and underachievement seem to be linked. Over half of children from Asian households are eligible for free school meals. Children who were eligible for free school meals are far less likely to achieve expected outcomes for Key Stages 1–4. Furthermore, African-Caribbean boys are three times more likely to be permanently excluded from school than white pupils.

e The student shows excellent knowledge and understanding of ways that poverty may impact upon the life-chances of ethnic minorities in the UK. The response demonstrates depth and breadth in understanding of a range of sociological material. Lots of relevant evidence is accurately cited. The student is awarded the full 12 marks for the skill of knowledge and understanding. The student shows an excellent ability to apply sociological knowledge explicitly and consistently throughout the response, and therefore is awarded the full 8 marks for this skill. **20/20 marks awarded.**

6 Sociologists generally accept that Britain is mainly stratified by social class, that is, it is divided into three broad socioeconomic strata or groups: the upper class, the middle classes and the working classes, who are differentiated from one another by the wealth they own, the jobs they have, the income they earn, the schools they go to and their cultural lifestyles. Marxists argue that the source of these social classes is the organisation and management of the capitalist system in which a minority of bourgeois business owners and employers exploit the labour-power of the working class and make huge profits and wealth. However, in addition to class inequalities, the UK experiences ethnic and gender inequalities, which has led to some critics suggesting that these inequalities are just as important as social class as a source of inequality.

e A promising opening paragraph in which the student intelligently notes the need to address all three concepts.

There is evidence that inequalities exist across ethnic groups in the UK, particularly between whites and ethnic minorities such as Pakistanis/Bangladeshis, and African-Caribbeans with regard to income, wealth and poverty. For example, Pakistanis and Bangladeshis are twice as likely to be living in long-term poverty compared with white people. They are also more likely to be unemployed, to be in low-paid jobs, to be in poor-quality and overcrowded rented accommodation and to be living in deprived, run-down, inner-city areas. Their children are more likely to be on free school meals. The link between poverty and underachievement at school is strong. Boys, particularly from Pakistani and African-Caribbean backgrounds, are likely to leave school at the age of 16 with very few qualifications. Boys from African-Caribbean backgrounds are three times more likely than working-class white boys to be excluded from school. This evidence therefore seems to suggest that ethnicity is a major source of inequality and that for black and Asian people it may be more important than social class.

e Excellent knowledge of a range of ethnic inequalities is demonstrated.

A similar argument is made by feminists who argue that gender is also a source of inequality which trumps social class. They point out that modern-day societies are patriarchal societies and that gender inequalities exist in a number of areas. For example, women tend to experience inequality at work in the form of vertical segregation. This means that their male colleagues are more likely to be promoted and that they are often paid less than men. Women therefore experience a glass ceiling — they can see the top jobs but male discrimination and prejudice prevent access to them despite equal opportunities laws. Consequently women are under-represented in a range of top jobs ranging from government ministers to judges to directors of top companies. Also, women are more likely to be found in low-paid temporary or insecure casual work compared with men.

Some feminist sociologists argue that this patriarchal discrimination has led to the feminisation of poverty because women generally do not earn as much as men because they are likely to be in low-status, low-skilled and part-time work. Moreover, many women cannot work because they are full-time carers of children, the sick and disabled, and the elderly. Many older women lack an occupational pension because of these domestic responsibilities.

ⓔ Excellent knowledge and understanding of a range of gender inequalities is shown.

> The evidence therefore seems to suggest that ethnicity and gender are important sources of inequality, but are they more important or just as important as social class? The first sociologist who tried to answer this question was Max Weber, who was critical of Karl Marx's argument that social class was the most important source of inequality, difference and conflict in society. However, although Weber agreed it was important, he argued it was just one type of status inequality that existed in modern societies. Weber pointed to examples of societies in which inequalities in wealth and income had nothing to do with work relationships and income, which is where social class originates. For example, there are societies in which factors such as religion (for example, India's caste system), membership of a political party (for example, the Nazis in Germany and the communists in the USSR), race (for example, apartheid South Africa or the segregated southern states of the USA) and military power (any society in which there has been a military coup or a dictator who uses force to get their way) are the major sources of status and therefore inequalities in power and wealth rather than social class. Weber also pointed out that even within social classes in capitalist societies there exist status differences based on skill which produce inequality. For example, the skilled working class earn more than the unskilled working class.
>
> These Weberian ideas led sociologists working in the fields of gender and ethnicity to suggest that even in the UK these social factors could work independently from social class to produce inequality in their own right. A good example of this is Barron and Norris's dual labour market theory, which sees the economy and workforce as divided into two sections. The primary sector is characterised by well-paid, highly skilled, secure jobs with plenty of opportunity for promotion. This sector is dominated by white workers. The secondary sector is characterised by low-paid, low-skilled, casual and insecure jobs. These jobs are mainly taken up by women and ethnic minorities. Access to the primary sector is controlled by white gate-keepers — employers and personnel officers — who discriminate against women and ethnic minorities and mainly allocate them to the secondary sector. Men and white people are also seen as generally responsible for the weak laws which exist to supposedly protect women and ethnic minorities from sexism and racism.

ⓔ This is a sophisticated account of Weber's ideas, which demonstrates excellent understanding. The examples used are very perceptive.

> These arguments have been challenged by Marxists. They see most ethnic minorities as members of the working class and therefore subject to the same objective economic experiences in terms of exploitation, low pay and appropriation of surplus value as the white working class. However, Marxists do acknowledge that these conditions are generally made worse

by racism. Miles, for example, identifies 'racialised class fractions' within the working class and middle classes. By this he means that although whites and ethnic minorities may share the same objective experience of work, they often occupy different social statuses to one another because white workers often used racial or ethnic differences to judge ethnic minorities as inferior. This was often used to justify racist practices such as trade union discrimination.

However, Marxists see racism as a capitalist ideology which is deliberately engineered and maintained by the capitalist class because it benefits in a number of ways. Firstly, the existence of a cheap ethnic minority workforce can be used to threaten the job security of the white working class and keep them in line. The ethnic minority workforce becomes a 'reserve army of labour' waiting in the wings, which prevents white workers demanding higher wages. Secondly, this 'threat' divides and rules the working class — if the white working class are convinced by racist beliefs that ethnic minorities are a threat to their jobs, neighbourhoods and communities then this plays off one section of the working class against another. Racism therefore has a scapegoating effect in that ethnic minorities are blamed for the problems of the white working class. This ensures that they do not unite against the capitalist class. It also distracts from the real cause of inequality — the organisation and management of the capitalist system.

e Excellent use of Marxism to evaluate Weber's ideas.

Feminists believe that patriarchy is more important than social class as a source of inequality for women. They point out that patriarchy existed well before capitalism came about and that it continued to persist in communist societies which had rid themselves of capitalism. However, Marxists argue that in capitalist societies, patriarchy is an ideological consequence of social class inequality. The Marxist-Feminist Benston argues that the bourgeoisie uses gender to divide and rule the male and female working class. Patriarchal ideology transmits the idea that women should be in the home, that their main task is to service their husbands and children, that jobs and careers are secondary to being a mother and so on.

Benston argues that this ideology is important because women's domestic labour is crucial to capitalism. It is women who reproduce and bring up the future workforce without any cost to the capitalist class. They also maintain the health and efficiency of the male workforce. Consequently, men are able to dominate the world of work and wield economic power over women. Women, on the other hand, are merely a reserve army of labour to be hired in low-paid casual jobs when the economy is doing well. When the economy goes into recession and they are fired, they simply return to their 'proper' jobs in the home.

ⓔ Another excellent summary of theory. It needed to be selective because the student could easily have got bogged down in the sheer volume of feminist material. However, they correctly focused on relevant aspects of Radical and Marxist-Feminism.

> In conclusion, then, although there are societies in which inequalities exist which have nothing to do with social class, in modern societies such as the UK, social class is an important source of inequalities in wealth and income. However, ethnicity and gender are important fault lines too, although Marxists argue that both racism and patriarchy are socially constructed as capitalist ideologies rather than independent influences on inequality.

ⓔ An intelligent conclusion is reached which sums up the debate fairly well. The student shows excellent knowledge and understanding of the relationship between class, gender and ethnicity, and theories of stratification. Sociological material was dealt with in depth and detail in an accurate fashion. However, the student surprisingly failed to identify and discuss class inequalities in income and wealth, although this was forgivable considering the scope of the debate. The student was therefore awarded 14 marks for knowledge and understanding. The full 8 marks were awarded for application because the response was always focused on the argument in the essay title. Evaluation, too, was generally excellent, although the student forgot to assess feminist perspectives. The student was awarded 13 marks for this skill. **35/40 marks awarded.**

ⓔ The student scored 92 marks out of the 105 available.

Question 2

Section A

Read the source material and answer all the questions in Section A.

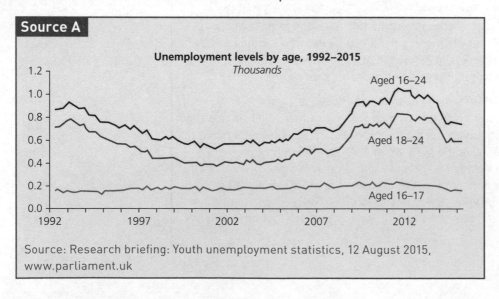

Source A

Unemployment levels by age, 1992–2015
Thousands

Aged 16–24

Aged 18–24

Aged 16–17

Source: Research briefing: Youth unemployment statistics, 12 August 2015, www.parliament.uk

Source B

The main aim of this report was to provide a better understanding of the reasons why some young men are able to overcome the impact of a period of long-term unemployment at an early stage in their careers while others face a future of recurrent unemployment and precarious employment.

A total of 32 biographical unstructured interviews, each lasting around 90 minutes, were conducted with men aged 25 to 29 years in a range of urban and rural areas. A non-random sampling technique was used by the researchers to ensure that those with extensive experience of unemployment were well represented. Many had multiple disadvantages (for example, residing in areas of high deprivation, coming from 'work-poor' families or having long-term health problems). The interviews were holistic in focus (covering labour market experiences from full-time employment to informal work, education, training, illegal activities, family, domestic and housing transitions), with the central concern being to identify the ways in which young men overcame the impact of long-term unemployment in their early careers or, conversely, the reasons why the impact of early experiences continued to affect their lives. The researchers also conducted interviews with 13 key officials who worked with young unemployed adults.

The study found that most of the young men who took part in the study were vulnerable workers. They had failed to thrive in a school environment for a number of reasons, and consequently they had left school at the earliest opportunity with few, if any, qualifications. Transitions from school to work were often turbulent and involved protracted (and usually repeated) periods of unemployment as well as time on schemes such as Youth Training. The majority of the sample were either in precarious forms of employment or were experiencing unemployment.

With most young men readily accepting any opportunity to work or train for new jobs, there was little evidence to suggest that the young men were feckless and preferred to live on benefits rather than work. The study also found that loss of self-confidence may prevent young people from applying for certain types of jobs and lead to a downgrading of expectations. It can affect performance at interviews.

From *Vulnerable young men in fragile labour markets: Employment, unemployment and the search for long-term security* by Furlong, A. and Cartmel, F., published in 2004 by the Joseph Rowntree Foundation. Reproduced by permission of the Joseph Rowntree Foundation.

1 Summarise the data shown in **Source A**. [4 marks]

e Don't forget to illustrate with examples.

2 With reference to **Source B**, explain **two** reasons why some sociologists use non-random sampling techniques when conducting sociological research. [6 marks]

e Don't forget to illustrate with reference to Source B.

3 With reference to **Source A**, explain **one** strength and **one** weakness of using official statistics to study youth unemployment over a period of time. [10 marks]

e Make sure each strength and weakness is detailed and is illustrated by a reference to Source A.

4 Using **Source B** and your wider sociological knowledge, assess the usefulness of questionnaires for investigating the everyday experience of youth unemployment. [25 marks]

e Describe the method and explain how it works in practice before describing and assessing its strengths and weaknesses.

Questions & Answers

Section B

Answer **all** the questions in Section B.

5 Outline ways in which poverty may impact upon young people's opportunities for social mobility.

[20 marks]

ℯ It is important to be detailed and to include reference to a reasonably wide range of ways.

6 'Stratification is functional for society.' Discuss.

[40 marks]

ℯ The word 'functional' should be a major clue as to the main focus of this essay. You will need to compare and contrast that theory with other theories of stratification.

Student answer

Section A

1 Source A refers to youth unemployment levels between 1992 and 2015. It suggests that unemployment rates for 16–17-year-olds have remained steadily low over this 23-year period. However, in contrast the number of 18–24-year-olds who were unemployed in 1993 was about 700,000, although this rose to about 800,000 in 2011–12, although this has fallen again to 600,000 in 2015. However, if these two age groups are added together, they totalled 900,000 in 1993 and rose to over a million in 2011–12, although this fell to 800,000 in 2015.

ℯ The student shows excellent ability by clearly and accurately summarising the data in Source A. **4/4 marks awarded.**

2 A suitable sampling frame, that is, a list of people who might take part in the study and who can be randomly sampled, is used in most survey research. However, in the case of the research in Source B, there was probably no official list of young unemployed men. The researchers were therefore forced to use a non-random sampling technique instead.

Random sampling techniques may not have produced people with the specific characteristics required whereas a non-random sampling technique such as purposive or opportunity sampling allows the researchers in Source B to directly approach people with the required characteristics, that is, unemployed men aged between 25 and 29 years old who lived in both urban and rural areas.

ℯ The student shows a clear understanding of two reasons why sociologists might use non-random sampling. A total of 2 marks are awarded for knowledge and understanding. The student also demonstrates an excellent ability to support knowledge with evidence from Source B and is awarded 4 marks for application. **6/6 marks awarded.**

3 Official statistics are advantageous in any study of youth unemployment over a period of time because the government operationalises the youth unemployment shown in Source A in a standardised and reliable way and therefore collects these statistics in the same way every year, which means that they are directly comparable. The trends and patterns therefore that can be identified can be regarded as valid.

However, such data can be both unreliable and invalid because sometimes governments change their definitions of youth and/or unemployment. These decisions are usually politically motivated and are aimed at giving the impression that youth unemployment has been successfully reduced by government policies. However, it does mean that the definitions of youth unemployment used by governments in Source A and sociologists may not be comparable.

ⓔ The student shows an excellent ability to apply data from Source A in answering the question. A total of 4 marks are therefore awarded for application. The student shows an excellent ability to evaluate official statistics to study youth unemployment in terms of both a strength and a weakness, and is awarded the full 6 marks. **10/10 marks awarded.**

4 Questionnaires are the main method of gathering large amounts of data from large numbers of people in social surveys. They are usually handed to people for self-completion or sent through the post. They are often made up of closed questions with fixed-choice tick-boxes attached which produce quantitative data.

ⓔ A promising beginning in that the student explains what a questionnaire is and describes how it might work in practice.

Questionnaires have a number of practical strengths. First, they can be distributed to very large samples of unemployed youth, which increases representativeness and the possibility of generalising to other young unemployed. Second, questionnaires are less time-consuming and costly than other methods. They can be sent out, returned and their results analysed very quickly. Third, questionnaires might be more useful than other methods for researching the effects of unemployment because some sections of the unemployed might be less willing to admit to depression, shame, crime and so on in face-to-face research.

Questionnaires tend to be ethically well managed. The aims and objectives of the research can be explained to those being asked to take part so that they can refuse or alternatively give informed consent. Moreover, most questionnaire surveys guarantee confidentiality — the information that the staff or patients give normally cannot be traced back to any one individual.

> Positivists are very keen on using survey questionnaires because they see them as scientific because they are thought to be objective and highly reliable. Another researcher using the same questionnaire on similar samples of unemployed young people should achieve similar results. Positivists also like the fact that questionnaires produce lots of quantitative data which can be compared, correlated and presented in table, chart or graph form.

ⓔ The above demonstrates excellent knowledge of questionnaires for sociological research purposes and convincingly outlines the theoretical reasons for their use. However, this section fails to make any reference to Source B. The research method in Source B needed to be compared with questionnaires.

> However, interpretivist sociologists have raised a number of practical, ethical and theoretical objections to questionnaires. First, it is practically difficult to go into any depth in a questionnaire. Most questionnaires use closed questions and fixed responses which don't allow the research subjects to discuss or explain their motivations or experiences. As the research in Source B illustrates, unstructured interviews are far more useful in this respect. Source B clearly shows that the interviewers were able to establish trust and rapport so that the interviewees openly talked about the turbulence they experienced during the transition from school to work, the downgrading of their expectations or their loss of self-confidence. It is unlikely that a questionnaire could have gathered such rich qualitative insight into how young men experience unemployment.
>
> Second, questionnaire research often suffers from non-response or low response which can undermine representativeness. The targeting of interviewees in Source B using purposive sampling meant that non-response was not a problem.
>
> Third, interpretivists believe that data collected by questionnaires lacks validity for two reasons. First, there is a danger that samples may interpret the same questions in different ways to that intended by the researcher, e.g. they may define the effects of unemployment in different ways. However, one of the advantages of using unstructured interviews in the research in Source B is that interviewers can make sure they achieve respondent validation by asking supplementary questions that probe motivations for behaving in particular ways.
>
> Second, interpretivists argue that questionnaires that use closed questions suffer from the 'imposition problem' — the researcher has already decided what experiences are important and included these in the questions and tick-box categories. If unemployed people are asked to fill in a questionnaire, they might feel that their experiences are not represented and either drop out of the research or tick categories that only approximate to their experience. The evidence collected therefore may lack validity.

e This section focuses confidently and convincingly on the practical and theoretical disadvantages of questionnaires. Very importantly, the student attempts to apply points made in Source B to this analysis.

> In contrast, the unstructured interviews used in Source B are likely to produce more highly valid data than the questionnaire about the effects of long-term unemployment because the interviewer is not restricted by a pre-set list of questions that impose experience on those being researched. Unstructured interviews can often result in unexpected findings compared with the questionnaire because the interviewee may tell the sociologist things the latter had not thought of — unstructured interviews therefore ensure that sociologists are open-minded and encourage the sociologist to learn as they go along.

e The student shows excellent knowledge and understanding of the nature, purpose and uses of questionnaire-based research. The response demonstrates some detail of a range of sociological material with some focus on sociological theory and concepts. The student was awarded the full 5 marks for knowledge and understanding. The student was awarded 3 marks for application because generally they showed a good ability to apply sociological theories and concepts to questionnaires. The student made some use of material both from the source and from elsewhere. The student was awarded 12 marks for evaluation because they demonstrated an excellent ability to evaluate and analyse the usefulness of questionnaires for investigating youth unemployment. The response included a range of explicit and relevant points evaluating questionnaires and made some comparison with other methodologies. **20/25 marks awarded.**

Section B

5 Poverty impacts on young people's opportunities for social mobility in a number of ways. First, there is evidence that child poverty is a major problem in the UK. According to official statistics, over a quarter of children were being brought up in low-income families in 2013. Such poverty has a number of consequences for these children. First, children born into poorer households often have a lower birth weight than children born into better-off families and consequently are at greater risk of infant mortality and chronic illness later on in life. Furthermore, these children are more likely to take time off school because they are more likely to become ill because of the poor state of the housing in which they often live. Second, as they grow up, poorer children may not experience the same life-chances as their better-off peers. For example, poverty means that they miss out on holidays, school trips, technology such as computers and so on because their parents cannot afford these 'luxuries'.

Third, the evidence suggests that poverty undermines schooling in that high-ability poor children do not attain the same level of qualifications as their better-off peers. For example, in 2011, children receiving free school meals, which is a sign of family poverty, achieved lower GCSE results than their wealthier peers. Fourth, poorer children are likelier to leave school at 16 and are more likely to be employed in precarious and casual low-skilled and low-paid work or to end up long-term unemployed. In 2015, the youth unemployment rate was nearly two and a half times higher than the overall unemployment rate, while nearly a quarter of a million 18–20-year-old workers earned the minimum wage.

Fifth, they may turn to crime and deviance out of boredom or to supplement their income. In some areas, they turn to gangs and/or drugs. They may find that they are subjected to more police attention, which creates hostility and the potential for urban disorder such as the 2011 London riots. Sixth, they are also more likely to become homeless as they lack the resources to get onto the property ladder. There is also evidence that poorer young people are dependent upon their parents for a greater length of time because the increase in the value of property combined with low pay and/or employment mean that it is virtually impossible for poorer young people to get on the property ladder.

In conclusion, then, poverty generally undermines meritocracy. Poor children do not have the same opportunities to better themselves compared with better-off children who have access to the economic, cultural and social capital provided by their parents.

e This is a detailed and convincing account of a wide range of effects resulting from the experience of poverty. The student shows excellent knowledge and understanding and explores its impact with a degree of depth and breadth. Evidence was cited, although it was slightly under-developed. The student therefore was awarded 10 marks for knowledge and 7 marks for application. **17/20 marks awarded.**

6 Functionalist and New Right sociologists believe that stratification is beneficial for society. Functionalists argue that class stratification existed because it was functional or beneficial to social order. They see modern societies as characterised by a specialised occupational division of labour, in which people have very different functions, skills and abilities. However, they argue that members of society are happy to take their place within this division of labour because there exists a value consensus about how society and its institutions such as work should be organised. This value consensus means that members of society accept that occupations should be graded in terms of their value to society and that those occupying the more functional or valued positions should receive greater rewards for their efforts.

The functionalists Davis and Moore argue that all societies have to ensure that their most important positions are filled with the most talented people if societies and particularly their economies are going to be successfully organised and managed. In order to do this, Davis and Moore insist that societies need to be meritocratic. This means that all members of society should enjoy equal opportunities to improve themselves through, for example, education. The most talented and skilled will rise to the top and take up jobs and responsibilities that most suit their qualities. High rewards in the form of income and status await those who make it to the top because gifted people need to be motivated and rewarded for the sacrifices involved in committing themselves to education and training. Furthermore, Davis and Moore argue that stratification encourages all members of society to work to the best of their ability because those at the top are motivated to hang onto their advantages of income and status while those occupying positions below them will wish to improve their social position.

Davis and Moore therefore argue that stratification is beneficial to society because it allocates all individuals to an occupational role that suits their abilities. They note that the majority are happy to accept this allocation to both occupational role and therefore social class because they believe that the means of allocation — educational qualifications and promotion on the basis of merit (talent, skill and hard work) — are fair.

e The above demonstrates excellent knowledge and understanding of the functionalist theory of stratification. It is detailed and uses concepts in a confident fashion.

However, Davis and Moore's account of stratification has been criticised on several counts. First, it is not clear how a job is defined as functional or essential to the effective running of society. Some jobs which can be described as essential such as nursing or in sanitation are not highly paid or accompanied by high status. Second, the notion of meritocracy is undermined by the ability of some sections of society to invest in private education and for occupational gate-keepers to favour the privately educated over other sections of society, despite the fact that the latter group may have better qualifications and greater talent. In a meritocracy there is a level playing field. There is little evidence that the UK is such a meritocracy when the children of the wealthy are disproportionately represented in the UK's top jobs because their families have more economic, cultural and social capital than everybody else. Other critics have also pointed out that those at the top of society are not financially rewarded by society for their position — rather, they award themselves incomes and they often fail to pay their fair share of taxes.

Third, Davis and Moore neglect the dysfunctions of stratification. In times of recession and austerity, unemployment and poverty can lead to great resentment towards those at the top of a stratified society, which can sometimes spill over into crime and urban disorder. Pickett and Wilkinson argue that as inequality has grown wider in societies such as the UK, so problems such as crime, suicide, mental illness and so on have also increased.

Questions & Answers

e The student demonstrates excellent knowledge in the two paragraphs above by perceptively considering a broad range of criticisms of functionalism in some depth.

However, despite these problems, functionalism has influenced New Right ideas about stratification. Saunders argues that capitalist societies have raised the standard of living for all members of society and therefore stratification and inequality are a small price to pay for such prosperity. Saunders argues that capitalism has to offer wealth incentives to those with talent, otherwise the technological progress that we have seen in the quality of consumer goods would not happen.

In contrast to the functionalist theory of stratification is Marxism, which argues that stratification only benefits a small minority — the capitalist class — and is actually harmful for the rest of society, particularly the working class.

Marx observed that UK society is a class society. The minority class — the bourgeoisie — owns the means of production (capital for investment, land, factories, technology and raw materials). The majority class — the proletariat — hires out its labour power to the bourgeoisie. This relationship between the bourgeoisie and the proletariat is known as the social relations of production. These relations are characterised by class inequality. The bourgeoisie exploit the labour power of the proletariat. They pay the lowest wages possible. Moreover, they pocket surplus value — the difference between the wage paid and the value the worker's labour has produced. Surplus value is the source of the wealth held by the capitalist class and, therefore, the cause of class inequalities in wealth which then lead to class inequalities in income, power, education, health and so on. In particular, it is the cause of the poverty that exists in the UK. Marxists therefore reject the notion that the UK is meritocratic. They argue instead that the system is loaded in favour of the rich and their children.

e Two alternative theories are considered as evaluative juxtaposition. The student looks at one which is supportive of the functionalist case while Marxism is considered because it takes an alternative stance.

Marx's theory of class conflict was an extremely influential theory, for example, it inspired revolutions in the USSR, China and Cuba — but it has been criticised. First, it has been argued that Marx's critique of capitalism may be over-stated — capitalism has a fairly good record in regard to democracy, workers' rights, the welfare state etc. Second, Weber criticised Marx for being an economic determinist — Marx sees social class as the most important source of inequality. However, Weber argued that there were other just as important sources, including gender/patriarchy, race/ethnicity, religion, military power and so on. Those who argue that patriarchal and ethnic inequalities exist independently of social class, such as Radical Feminists, would agree with Weber. Finally, Marx has been criticised by postmodernists who argue that social class is no longer an important aspect of identity today. Pakulski and Waters argued that social class is now dead and that other criteria such as consumption choices or cleavages, globalisation and social media are more important in the construction of personal identity. However, in defence of Marx, social attitude surveys, especially those conducted by Savage, suggest that people still categorise themselves according to social class criteria.

e Excellent evaluative knowledge of Marxism is demonstrated.

This student has shown impressive knowledge of functionalism and other theories of stratification throughout. The student uses concepts and applies theory confidently and with perception. It is difficult to see how this particular piece of work could be improved in the time allocated. The student, quite rightly, saw the need to apply evaluation throughout to all the major outlined theories. **40/40 marks awarded.**

e Overall the student scored 97 marks out of a possible 105 for this paper.

Question 3

Section A

Read the source material and answer all the questions in Section A.

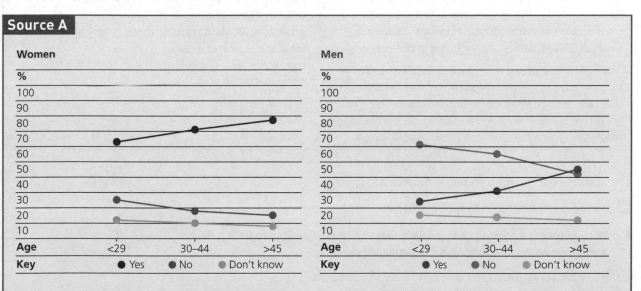

Source A

Response to the question 'Do you believe there are still barriers to women progressing to top levels of management (a glass ceiling)?'

These data were collected via an online survey of 2,960 members of the Institute of Leadership and Management, almost equally divided between men (49%) and women (51%).

Source: Ambition and gender at work, Institute of Leadership and Management, 2013, www.tinyurl.com/oten4y6

Source B

The Intergenerational Social Mobility of Minority Ethnic Groups by Lucinda Platt (2005)

This study considers two key variables in social mobility: social class of origin and ethnicity. In particular, it explores the relationship between social class and ethnicity in an attempt to measure their relative influence on the opportunities for upward social mobility for the children of ethnic minority and migrant parents.

The study was based on data collected by the Office for National Statistics (ONS) Longitudinal Study. The ONS Longitudinal Study (LS) is a 1% sample of the population of England and Wales that is followed over time. It was initially obtained by taking a sample of the 1971 census, based on those born on one of four birth dates (day and month). For this study, two cohorts of children aged between four and 15 at the point they were observed in the LS have been selected from both the 1971 and the 1981 records in the LS. Their parents' and household characteristics are measured at that point to give information about their 'origins', and their own characteristics are measured in 2001 to given information about their 'destinations'. Altogether over 50,000 people were included in the research.

The results showed that in absolute terms, some ethnic minority groups ended up in a better position than others. For example, Indians did better than all other groups considered, although the fact that many Indian children came from middle-class backgrounds played a role in their outcome, which suggests that class matters. However, ethnicity appears to be more of an influential factor for Pakistanis because their children found it more difficult to escape from their parents' working-class origins. The data suggested that racial inequality may be a factor preventing upward social mobility for the children of this group because white working-class children were more likely to experience upward social mobility.

The research also found that Caribbeans, black Africans, Indians, Chinese and others, and white migrants all obtained upward mobility relative to white non-migrants, taking their origins into account. They had higher chances than their white non-migrant counterparts of ending up in the professional or managerial classes, when comparing like with like. This indicates that society may be relatively open to minority ethnic groups.

However, the data does suggest that class advantage is still more important than ethnicity as a cause of upward mobility. Parents who were middle-class professionals were able to ensure greater educational success for their children because they had access to social networks and they were able to equip their children with the necessary cultural capital.

Adapted from *Migration and social mobility: The life-chances of Britain's minority ethnic communities* by Lucinda Platt (2005), Joseph Rowntree Foundation.

---

1 **Summarise the data shown in Source A.** [4 marks]

ⓔ Don't forget to illustrate with examples.

2 **With reference to Source B, explain two reasons why sociologists use sampling when conducting sociological research.** [6 marks]

ⓔ Don't forget to illustrate with reference to Source B.

3 **With reference to Source A, explain one strength and one weakness of using online surveys to research the effect of gender on career ambitions.** [10 marks]

ⓔ Make sure each strength and weakness is detailed and is illustrated by a reference to Source A.

4 Using **Source B** and your wider sociological knowledge, assess the usefulness of longitudinal survey data to research the social mobility of minority ethnic groups. [25 marks]

e Describe the method and explain how it works in practice before describing and assessing its strengths and weaknesses.

Section B

Answer **all** the questions in Section B.

5 Outline ways in which women may experience both horizontal and vertical segregation in the workplace. [20 marks]

e It is important to be detailed and to include reference to a reasonably wide range of ways.

6 'Patriarchal inequality is the result of one class — men — exploiting the labour power of another class — women.' Discuss. [40 marks]

e You will need to work out which feminist theory is being quoted in the title. You will need to outline its ideas in detail and compare these with other feminist and non-feminist theories.

Student answer

Section A

1 Source A shows how men and women members of the Institute of Leadership and Management feel about the glass ceiling. The graph for women shows that between 70% and 80% of female members across the age range 29–45 believe that barriers exist which prevent women progressing to the top levels of management. Older women were more likely to believe this than younger women. In contrast, the graph for men suggests that men are less likely to believe that a glass ceiling exists. However, older men more so than younger men were prepared to believe such barriers exist.

e The student shows excellent ability by clearly and accurately summarising the data in Source A. **4/4 marks awarded.**

2 First, it is sometimes practically impossible to survey the whole population of a group that a sociologist wants to investigate because the group may number thousands or more. A representative sample which has the same social characteristics of the wider population is usually selected instead using a random sampling method.

Second, the sociologist may not have the practical resources to carry out research on big populations. Sampling saves both time and expense because sociologists may not have either the time or money to carry out large-scale research.

Questions & Answers

e The reasons why sampling is used are well explained but the student forgets to make reference to Source B to help illustrate the points made. Consequently, they are awarded the full 2 marks for knowledge and understanding but score 0 from the 4 available for application of Source B. **2/6 marks awarded.**

> **3** If a questionnaire is posted on a specific website such as the Institute of Leadership and Management aimed at people who have direct experience of the research topic, and who access that website frequently, it is likely to lead to a fairly high response rate. The individuals who use this site are likely to be highly relevant to the research. Using such a site is a good example of purposive sampling.
>
> However, if a questionnaire is posted on a less specific website, say the BBC, there is a danger that both those who complete the questionnaire and the responses to it may be biased. The research may attract those who already have a vested interest in the research topic, for example women who feel they have been the victims of employer discrimination rather than women workers in general. Also, the anonymity of the internet means that some people, especially men, might be tempted to sabotage the research by posting spoof responses.

e This response does all that is required. It demonstrates an excellent ability to apply data from Source A in answering the question. There is a clear application of source material in relation to both the strength and the weakness identified. Consequently, it is awarded the full 4 marks for application and the full 6 marks for evaluation. **10/10 marks awarded.**

> **4** Longitudinal surveys are those which are carried out over a period of years. They are often carried out by government departments because individual sociologists and research charities often do not have the practical resources to carry out such time-consuming and costly research. Consequently, the data from such surveys are usually expressed in the form of official statistics.
>
> The research in Source B carried out by Platt was based on a government survey called the Office for National Statistics Longitudinal Survey (LS), which itself was based on data collected by the censuses of 1971, 1981 and 2001. The census is a government questionnaire which has to be completed by every household in the UK. Platt was able to study the class origin and destination of over 50,000 parents and their children using this data.
>
> The use of official statistics is attractive to sociologists for several reasons. First, they are a cheap source of data because the government has carried out the expensive task of collecting them. Second, they are often very contemporary and readily available via government websites and publications. Third, they often cover very large samples and consequently they are usually representative of particular social groups or, in the case of the census, of everyone. This is particularly useful because it means that they have comparative value. Sociologists can compare particular

groups, for example, in Source B ethnic minority groups, in order to uncover correlations, for example in the case of Source B between social class and ethnicity. Fourth, they can be used to assess the success or failure of government social policy or trends and patterns over a long period of time, for example in the case of Source B, over a 30-year period.

Fifth, official statistics often avoid the pitfalls of primary research methods. For example, they are attractive to sociologists because they involve no direct contact with people and therefore the sociologist does not have to pay attention to ethical issues such as informed consent, deception etc. They are also regarded as objective because the sociologist does not have to worry about interviewer or observer effects.

A sixth strength of official statistics is the fact that they are usually collected by government questionnaire surveys such as the census which are designed in a highly scientific way, and which according to positivist sociologists are standardised, systematic, objective and reliable in practice. Another researcher using the same questionnaire on similar samples of people should achieve similar results. Positivists also argue that government questionnaires produce highly valid data because everyone is exposed to the same stimuli in the sense that everyone is answering the same questions, therefore any difference in responses should truly reflect differences in real life.

In Source B, these strengths helped Platt collect information about the relative chances of ethnic groups, particularly ethnic minority groups, to achieve upward social mobility. For example, she was able to conclude that Indians were more likely to achieve upward social mobility than Pakistanis. However, she was also able to show that advantages and disadvantages associated with social class meant that the children of ethnic minorities who had professional jobs were more likely to achieve upward social mobility than the children of those in manual jobs.

However, some sociologists argue that official statistics have limitations that might affect Platt's conclusions in Source B. First, they may be based on operational definitions that sociologists would not agree with. For example, sociologists would need to make sure that the way that the government defined and measured social class was in agreement with sociological definitions and measurements. Second, interpretivists argue that statistics tell sociologists very little about the human stories or interpretations that underpin them. For example, with regard to Source B, statistics do not document the everyday experience of supporting children through education or the experience of racism. Third, all questionnaires, including the census, are artificial devices which are not a normal part of everyday reality — people may therefore respond to them with suspicion, i.e. they may feel that any information they write on the questionnaire may be used against them in some way and consequently they may respond with evasive, partial or false, and therefore invalid, information. Fourth, there is no guarantee that respondents to official questionnaires interpret questions in the same way, which undermines both the reliability of the method and the validity of the data.

Questions & Answers

e The student is awarded the full 5 marks for knowledge because the response clearly shows a perceptive, detailed and accurate understanding of the nature, purpose and uses of longitudinal research. The student scored the full 5 marks for application because they applied sociological theories, concepts and evidence to their analysis. The student explicitly applied material both from the source and from elsewhere. Evaluation, too, was first class, both from a practical and a theoretical point of view. The student was awarded the full 15 marks for this skill. **25/25 marks awarded.**

Section B

5 Horizontal segregation essentially means that men and women are concentrated into different types of jobs in different sectors of the economy. If we examine the public sector, that is, government jobs, the statistics suggest women make up over 70% of those employed in health and education. In the private sector, women are disproportionately concentrated in clerical, administrative, retail and personal services such as catering, whereas men are mainly found in the skilled manual and upper professional sectors.

Vertical gender segregation means that women are more likely than men to occupy the lower-status levels of an occupation and to be paid less (despite equal opportunities legislation). Furthermore, when women have gained access to the upper professional or management sector, they may encounter a 'glass ceiling' — they can climb the ladder so far but then they encounter barriers whereby they can see where they want to go but cannot climb any further. Consequently, women workers are under-represented in top jobs such as directors of companies, judges, newspaper editors, chief constables, surgeons and so on. Feminist sociologists claim that the glass ceiling is caused by discrimination by employers who are reluctant to invest in female employees because they subscribe to stereotypes about women taking time off work to have children.

Another aspect of vertical segregation is pay. The evidence in 2015 indicates that there is a 19% difference in terms of gross hourly pay between men and women. The Equal Opportunities Commission (EOC) concludes that women earn significantly less than men, whether they are lawyers or sales assistants, and that women as a whole are unlikely to achieve earning parity with men until 2040. Again, feminists claim that gender discrimination is responsible for this, although Hakim argues that women often make rational choices to commit themselves to family at the expense of career. Consequently, women are more likely to occupy part-time jobs as well as temporary casual work, which are both low-paid. Part-time work tends to have worse working conditions, less job security and fewer promotion prospects than full-time work.

e With regard to knowledge and understanding, the full 12 marks are awarded because the student shows excellent knowledge and understanding of ways that horizontal and vertical segregation affects the lives of women. The response demonstrates depth and detail and uses sociological evidence and concepts in convincing and confident fashion. The student is awarded the full 8 marks for application because the response is focused on the two concepts throughout. **20/20 marks awarded.**

---

5 The idea that patriarchal inequality is the result of men as a class exploiting the labour power of the class of women is a feminist one. However, there are a number of different feminist perspectives and consequently some debate about how patriarchal the UK actually is. All feminist theories of society see modern capitalist societies as patriarchal or male dominated. They argue that the social institutions that make up society, such as the family, education, mass media, religion and the economy, function to bring about a social system in which men dominate economic and social power while women mainly dominate subordinate positions.

---

e A good introduction which sets the scene for the debate about patriarchal inequality.

Radical Feminists see the organisation of all societies — whether they are capitalist or not — as patriarchal and consequently resulting in gender inequalities. They see a fundamental conflict between men and women who they categorise as 'sex-classes'. They argue that patriarchy existed well before capitalism appeared in the eighteenth century. Furthermore, they argue that patriarchy benefits all men. Kate Millett and Shula Firestone argue that men and women have very different interests, and that men exploit women in all aspects of social life. They argue that family, government, cultural traditions, religion, law, education and the media all reflect and transmit patriarchal ideology, especially the idea that it is normal and natural for men to have power and for women to be in a supporting and subordinate role.

Radical Feminists believe that patriarchy begins in the family because gender role socialisation is where children learn that men and women are not only biologically different but that they should occupy separate and distinct social roles, too. Girls learn that their role is secondary to that of males and that their lives should be dedicated primarily to servicing men, home and family. Radical Feminists also believe that all men benefit in various ways from the general exploitation of women. For example, Delphy and Leonard argue that husbands (even when they love their wives) exploit women in the home by making little contribution to housework and childcare. Women are expected to be there for men, to flatter them, to physically, sexually and emotionally maintain them etc. Patriarchal ideology is used to control women for the benefit of men. Women are told how to look, dress and behave. When patriarchal ideology fails, then women are subjected to the threat of male violence and sexual aggression, which limits their capacity to live as free and independent beings.

---

e The two paragraphs above intelligently lay out the Radical Feminist argument in a cogent, perceptive and impressive way. Concepts and studies are used very well in support.

> However, the Radical Feminist perspective has been challenged by Marxist-Feminists, who see the organisation of capitalist societies as primarily resulting in both social class inequalities and patriarchal inequalities. Marxist-Feminists see capitalist society as deliberately constructing conflict between men and women in order to distract from the more important social class inequalities caused by capitalist exploitation.

e A pertinent criticism is raised but the student misses the necessary opportunity to explore Marxist-Feminism. This is puzzling because Marxist-Feminists provide an important account of the reasons for patriarchy. Benston's work in particular is crucial.

> Walby has attempted to combine the ideas of Radical and Marxist theory. She argues that women are exploited by both capitalism and patriarchy. She argues that there are two types of patriarchy — private and public. She argues that patriarchy interacts with capitalism and racism to produce a modern form of gender stratification underpinned by six types of inequality specifically located in the economy, family, state policies and laws, mass media representations, personal relationships and men's use of violence.

e This paragraph sounds impressive but it lacks illustration. The distinction between private and public forms of patriarchy needs to be made clear. It is also vague about what form the six types of patriarchy take in practice.

> Another feminist perspective is Liberal Feminism, which argues that patriarchy and therefore gender inequalities are caused by two factors. First, Ann Oakley blames gender role socialisation. Second, men dominate the worlds of work, politics, law, religion and this means they were able to build economic and cultural barriers which prevented women from achieving equality. However, Liberal Feminists argue that women's position in UK society is improving and that the influence of patriarchy is in decline.

e It is good that this student has seen the need to include Liberal Feminism, but this account is a bit vague and therefore disappointing. It raises more questions than it answers. For example, why is gender role socialisation to blame? What political and cultural barriers have men raised? Why is patriarchy in decline?

> However, Liberal Feminists acknowledge that there is still some distance to go towards full equality between men and women. They are still concerned that some patriarchal inequalities such as domestic violence continue to persist.
>
> Feminists in general have been criticised as over-deterministic because they suggest that men and women's social behaviour is wholly shaped by patriarchal influences. However, Hakim's research suggests some women

may be quite happy to be mothers and housewives — they actively and rationally choose this option. Other critics have suggested that patriarchy may be the product of women's reproductive role — biology — rather than gender role socialisation, patriarchal culture or capitalism. Feminists also neglect the many divisions between women on grounds of income and social class, ethnicity and religion. For example, black or Asian women may experience more male exploitation than white women. Educated middle-class women with careers and a good income may be able to resist male exploitation. Scott argues that support for gender equality is declining across Britain because people now believe that both the mother and the family will suffer if a woman works full-time.

This is quite a good collection of evaluative points, although again there is a tendency towards vagueness. The student is awarded 11 marks for knowledge and understanding because although most of the content was relevant, it was often superficial and vague. However, the student did understand what they were writing about and used concepts well. There needed to be more illustrative evidence. The student was awarded 6 marks for application. The exclusion of any examination of Marxist-Feminism and the implicit nature of large sections of the answer showed a lack of focus. The student was awarded 11 marks for evaluation. Some excellent points were raised, especially with regard to feminism in general, and there was evaluative juxtaposition, too. **28/40 marks awarded.**

Altogether this student is awarded 89 marks out of a possible 105.

Knowledge check answers

1 Very little research is repeated and verified by other sociologists because there is little reward or status to be gained from re-doing other people's research.

2 Social forces or laws which originate in the way societies are organised, such as class, consensus and so on.

3 People have free will and therefore choose to act and organise themselves in the way that they do.

4 Interpretivist methods are often dependent on establishing a personal relationship with research subjects which other sociologists might find difficult to repeat and verify.

5 People or groups who pay for research might expect findings that generally confirm their world view.

6 Some subject matter is sensitive, embarrassing and so on and consequently people may lie or be partial with the truth in response.

7 Interpretivists prefer qualitative data.

8 Interpretivists are more likely to adopt respondent validation.

9 Positivists tend to believe that sociologists should be objective pursuers of truth and therefore should not have to take responsibility for how their data is used by governments.

10 Marxism and feminism want to change the world for the better.

11 People who respond to research via the internet may not be representative of the group being studied because they may have a vested and biased interest in the research topic. For example, a study of religious belief is more likely to attract those with a strong commitment to religion rather than ordinary people.

12 Positivists prefer the use of the survey questionnaire.

13 The structured interview is based on a questionnaire, which is read out word for word by the interviewer.

14 The interviewer has to follow the questionnaire faithfully and is rarely allowed scope for asking follow-up questions which might explore motives and so on.

15 Official statistics are collected by people and may therefore tell sociologists more about their prejudices and biases. For example, crime statistics collected by the police may reflect police prejudice against young people or ethnic minorities, which results in them being stopped more frequently in the street.

16 Wealth refers to assets such as property and the contents of bank accounts. It can be inherited or accumulated as a result of savings, rents, investments and profits. Income refers to wages or salaries which are earned from jobs.

17 Private schools are extremely expensive and out of the reach of ordinary people. For example, the 2015 fees for Eton College were more than £30,000 per year yet the average annual wage in the UK was £26,000.

18 Employers apply the motherhood penalty to women workers.

19 Pakistanis and Bangladeshis are over-represented in semiskilled jobs such as taxi driving because it is semiskilled work in which men from these ethnic groups are over-represented. Sociologists are divided as to whether this is due to white employers denying them access to better paid jobs or whether these jobs fit their educational profile, e.g. Pakistanis and Bangladeshis are less likely to have A-level and degree qualifications. They may choose to work for employers who are Pakistani or Bangladeshi.

20 Employers may prefer to employ white people rather than members of ethnic minorities.

21 A meritocracy is a society in which people are rewarded solely on the basis of talent, skill and hard work.

22 Poverty, crime, riots, lack of community spirit and the envy and hostility created by inequality are examples of the dysfunctions of stratification.

23 The infrastructure is the capitalist economic system in which the capitalist class exploits the labour power of the working class.

24 The superstructure functions to transmit ruling-class ideology, which operates to convince the working class that the capitalist system is fair and meritocratic so that inequality is rarely criticised or challenged.

25 Economic reductionism involves always reducing the causes of inequality to social class, which originates in the economic system.

26 Weber categorises social class as just another type of status inequality.

27 A reserve army of labour is an easily exploitable group of workers drawn from vulnerable groups who can be moved in and out of the labour market as it suits capitalists.

28 Liberal Feminism is more optimistic because it sees patriarchy as being in decline whereas Radical Feminism does not.

29 She is critical of feminist approaches because (a) they dismiss the mother–housewife role as inferior to paid work and (b) they neglect women's rational choices to be mother–housewives.

Index